Set,
Simmer, &
Savour It!

Set, Simmer, & Savour It!

**More Than 75 Easy Recipes
for the Slow Cooker**

Compiled by Anne Sheasby

SALAMANDER

A Salamander Book

Published by Salamander Books Ltd.

8 Blenheim Court

Brewery Road

London N7 9NY

United Kingdom

© Salamander Books Ltd., 2003

A member of **Chrysalis** Books plc

ISBN 1 84065 492 9

1 3 5 7 9 8 6 4 2

Credits

Project Manager: Anne McDowall

Commissioning Editor: Stella Caldwell

Designers: twelveotwo

Production: Ian Hughes

Color reproduction: Anorax Imaging Ltd.

Printed in China

The recipes in this book have appeared in previous Salamander titles by other authors and have been compiled by Anne Sheasby and edited by Anne McDowall for this edition.

Notes

All spoon measurements are level: 1 teaspoon = 5ml spoon; 1 tablespoon = 15ml spoon

Contents

Introduction

Although they have been around for years, slow cookers are only now making a well-deserved comeback. Slow-cooking is the perfect way to prepare a wide variety of delicious food, from soups and stews to fondues and fruit compotes, and it's hard to beat the aroma of a delicious casserole, perfectly cooked and ready to eat, when you arrive home at the end of a tiring day!

Slow cookers are simple and economical to use and require little or no attention once the ingredients for your recipe have been prepared ready for cooking. Foods are usually cooked for long periods of time, so ingredients such as meat – even the cheapest, toughest cuts – and vegetables become deliciously tender. Slow cooking also retains all the goodness and develops the flavour of foods. There is little evaporation, so food doesn't dry out.

Choosing a slow cooker

A good selection of slow cookers is widely available, many at a modest price, in a range of shapes and colours and varying in capacity from approximately 1.5 litres (2½ pints) to 5 or 6 litres (5 or 6 quarts). All slow cookers operate at a low wattage and consume a similar amount of electricity and the efficient insulation built into the appliance ensures that only the food inside the cooker heats up and not the whole kitchen.

There are two main types of slow cooker. The most common ones have a removable inner earthenware or ceramic cooking pot. The outer casing of these models is usually made of metal or heat-resistant plastic and is fitted with an inner metal casing. The removable cooking pot sits in the inner casing and the heating elements are situated between the inner and outer casings. Lids are made of heat-resistant glass or ceramic.

Other less common types comprise an earthenware or ceramic pot that is permanently fixed into an outer casing. The heating elements are housed between the outer casing and the cooking pot.

Using a slow cooker

Always read through the manufacturer's instructions before using your slow cooker for the first time. Models vary slightly and even on the same setting, some will cook faster or slower than others. Use your slow cooker several times before trying the recipes in this book; the timings given are intended to be an accurate guide, but you may find that your model cooks more quickly or more slowly and that you need to adjust the cooking times accordingly.

Most slow cookers have three basic settings – OFF, LOW and HIGH; others also include an AUTO setting. Most models have a power indicator light. On the LOW setting, the slow cooker will cook foods very gently with hardly any simmering. On the HIGH setting, the cooker may actually boil some foods and liquids. With the AUTO setting, cooking starts at a high temperature, then automatically switches to a LOW cook and the temperature is thermostatically controlled. Most of the recipes in this book use the HIGH or LOW settings.

The slow cooker may need to be preheated on HIGH for about 20 minutes (refer to the manufacturer's instructions for your specific model). You can often use this time to prepare the ingredients for cooking. To preheat your slow cooker (if applicable), simply place the empty cooking pot in the slow cooker base, place the lid in position, plug in and switch on with the control set on HIGH. Once the cooker is preheated, add the prepared ingredients to the cooking pot, replace the lid and continue cooking as directed in the recipe.

Adapting your own recipes

Once you are used to using your slow cooker, you will easily be able to adapt your own recipes to cook in the slow cooker. Simply refer to similar recipes in this book or in the manufacturer's handbook and change cooking times accordingly.

It is also worth remembering, however, that because there is less evaporation in a slow cooker, you will almost always need to reduce the quantity of liquid used. In a slow cooker, steam condenses on the lid and returns to the pot and, in doing so, forms a seal around the lid that retains heat and flavour.) As a guide, use about half the quantity of liquid given in a conventional recipe – you can always add a little more boiling liquid at the end of the cooking time if the cooked result is too thick. If you wish to reduce the quantity of liquid at the end of the cooking time, remove the lid after cooking, turn the setting to HIGH and reduce by simmering for an additional 30-45 minutes.

Tips for slow cooking

- Unless the recipe specifies otherwise, do not lift the lid during the cooking process, as this will break the water seal around the rim and will interfere with the cooking time. (With most recipes, there is no need to turn or stir the food, as it will not stick, burn or bubble over, and slow cooking provides a very even method of cooking.)
- If you do need to lift the lid while cooking, remember to increase the cooking time by about 20-30 minutes in order to allow the slow cooker to regain lost heat.
- If you need to speed up the cooking process, simply switch the control to the HIGH setting. As an approximate guide, the cooking time on HIGH is just over half of that on LOW.
- Dishes to be cooked in a slow cooker should always contain some liquid.
- When cooking joints of meat or foods that are cooked in dishes such as pudding basins, ensure that the food or dish fits comfortably in the cooking pot and that the lid fits securely before you begin to prepare the recipe.
- Ideally slow cookers should be filled to a maximum of 1-2.5cm ($\frac{1}{2}$-1in) from the top of the cooking pot. Make sure that the cooking pot is at least half full and no more than three-quarters full.
- Once cooking time is complete, you can keep food hot by switching the setting to LOW.
- If at the end of cooking time the food is not ready, replace the lid, switch the setting to HIGH and continue cooking for an additional 30-60 minutes, or until the food is thoroughly cooked.
- With dishes such as soups and casseroles, once the cooking time is complete, always stir the dish well before serving.
- Cakes cooked in a slow cooker do not brown in the way that they do when baked in a conventional oven, so they are often paler in colour – though they taste just as good! Icing spread on top of a cooked cake, or sugar or nuts sprinkled over the top of it, will improve its appearance.
- Where a recipe for a cake or dessert calls for a cake tin, always use one with a fixed/non-removable base (rather than a loose-based or springform one).
- Cold cooked food should not be reheated in the slow cooker, as it will not reach a high enough temperature to be safe.

Slow cookers with removable cooking pots are more versatile than those in which the pot is permanently fixed into an outer casing.

Preparing food for slow cooking

Trim excess fat from meat and cut meat into small, even, bite-sized pieces. Cut vegetables, especially root vegetables, into small dice or thin slices. (Surprisingly, vegetables often take longer to cook than meat in a slow cooker.) Place the diced vegetables in the base or towards the bottom half of the cooking pot and ensure that they are covered completely with liquid.

You can speed up the cooking a little by precooking vegetables in oil or butter in a pan to soften before adding them to the slow cooker. Pre-browning or sealing meat in oil or melted butter in a pan before adding it to the slow cooker also improves the appearance, texture and flavour of the cooked food. It is often a good idea to bring the cooking liquid to the boil before adding it to the slow cooker.

If you don't have time to precook vegetables or meat, preheat the slow cooker on HIGH while preparing the ingredients. Place the chopped vegetables in the base of the cooking pot, add the meat or poultry, then add herbs or seasonings and pour over enough boiling stock or liquid to just cover the food. Switch the setting to LOW and cook as instructed – you will need to add about 2-3 hours to the minimum recommended cooking time.

Food to be slow cooked should be seasoned lightly with salt and pepper, especially salt. Add the minimum amount of salt and then check and adjust the seasoning before serving.

Always defrost frozen ingredients thoroughly before placing them in a slow cooker. Defrosted frozen vegetables are usually added towards the end of the cooking time.

Soak dried beans in plenty of cold water for at least 10 hours or overnight, then drain, place in a large pan, cover with fresh cold water and boil for 10 minutes. Drain them and use as required. Red kidney beans should be boiled rapidly for 10 minutes, to kill any toxins present. Lentils do not need precooking. Use easy/quick-cooking varieties of rice and pasta.

To avoid separation or curdling, dairy products, such as cream and milk, are best added towards the end of the cooking time – or at the end of cooking, if possible. Use whole (full-fat/full-cream) milk, rather than semi-skimmed or skimmed milk.

Use dried herbs rather than fresh. Dried herbs tend to create a better flavour during the long, slow cooking process. (To further enhance the flavour and appearance of a dish, you can stir chopped fresh herbs into the finished dish or sprinkle them on top, if desired.)

Caring for and cleaning a slow cooker

◆ Refer to the manufacturer's guidelines about caring for and cleaning your slow cooker.

◆ Do not subject the cooking pot to sudden changes in temperature and never plunge it into cold or boiling water.

◆ Do not leave the pot immersed in water as this may adversely affect the porous base.

◆ Remove any stubborn stains with a soft brush or nylon cleaning pad. Do not use abrasive cleaners or scourers on the cooking pot or outer casing of your slow cooker.

◆ The outer casing of the slow cooker should never be immersed in water, filled with liquid or food or used for cooking without the inner cooking pot. To clean, wipe the outer casing with a cloth soaked in warm, soapy water.

◆ Most cooking pots and lids are not suitable for washing in a dishwasher and many cannot be placed in an oven, freezer or microwave or on a conventional hob – check the manufacturer's instructions for your model.

◆ After cooking, always use oven gloves to remove the cooking pot from the slow cooker base (and when removing the lid), as the pot (and lid) will be hot.

Soups and Starters

Roasted Tomato Soup with Coriander

SERVES 4

900G (2LB) RIPE PLUM TOMATOES

115ML (4FL OZ) OLIVE OIL

1 TABLESPOON CHOPPED
FRESH THYME

2 TEASPOONS GRATED LEMON ZEST

1 LEEK, FINELY CHOPPED

2 GARLIC CLOVES, CHOPPED

1 TABLESPOON GROUND CORIANDER

150ML (5FL OZ) WHITE WINE

115G (4OZ) DAY-OLD WHITE BREAD

950ML (30FL OZ) VEGETABLE STOCK

2 TABLESPOONS CHOPPED
FRESH CORIANDER

1 TABLESPOON LEMON JUICE

◆ Preheat oven to 230°C(450°F/Gas 8). Quarter tomatoes and place in one layer on a large baking sheet. Drizzle over 4 tablespoons oil and sprinkle over thyme, lemon zest and some sea salt. Roast for 30 minutes until tomatoes are charred and very mushy.

◆ Preheat the slow cooker on HIGH. Heat 2 tablespoons oil in a saucepan and sauté leek, garlic and coriander for 5 minutes. Add wine and boil for 3 minutes.

◆ Remove and discard crusts from bread and crumble. Add bread, tomatoes and stock and bring to the boil. Transfer to the cooking pot, cover, reduce temperature to LOW and cook for 4-6 hours.

◆ Cool slightly, purée, then return to rinsed-out cooking pot, cover and cook on LOW for 30-60 minutes, or until hot.

◆ Blend remaining oil, fresh coriander and lemon juice together and drizzle over soup. Serve with warm Italian bread, if desired.

Potato and Garlic Soup with Pesto

SERVES 4-6

2 HEADS GARLIC

1.2 LITRES (2 PINTS)
VEGETABLE STOCK

1 BAY LEAF

2 PARSLEY AND 2 THYME SPRIGS

2 TABLESPOONS OLIVE OIL

1 ONION, CHOPPED

1 TEASPOON GROUND CUMIN

700G (1½LB) FLOURY POTATOES,
PEELED AND DICED

4-6 TABLESPOONS PESTO, TO SERVE

◆ Preheat slow cooker on HIGH for 15 minutes. Separate garlic cloves, peel and place in a saucepan with stock and ½ teaspoon sea salt. Tie bay leaf, parsley and thyme in a piece of muslin and add to pan. Bring to boil, transfer to cooking pot, cover and cook on HIGH for 1-2 hours. Discard muslin bag and make stock up to 1.2 litres (2 pints) with water.

◆ Heat oil in a large clean saucepan and sauté onion and cumin for 5 minutes. Add potatoes and sauté for 5 minutes. Pour in garlic broth and bring to boil. Transfer to rinsed-out cooking pot, cover, reduce to LOW and cook for 6-8 hours or until vegetables are cooked and tender.

◆ Cool slightly, then purée soup in a blender or food processor. Season to taste, return to the cooking pot and cook on LOW for 30-60 minutes.

◆ Spoon soup into bowls and stir a tablespoon of pesto into each.

Parsnip Soup with Nutmeg

SERVES 4-6

2 TABLESPOONS OLIVE OIL

450G (1LB) PARSNIPS,
CUT INTO CHUNKS

1 LARGE POTATO, CUT INTO CHUNKS

1 LARGE ONION, CHOPPED

950ML (30FL OZ)
VEGETABLE STOCK

SALT AND GROUND BLACK PEPPER

2 TABLESPOONS
GREEK-STYLE YOGURT

LARGE PINCH FRESHLY
GRATED NUTMEG

GREEK-STYLE YOGURT AND FRESHLY
GRATED NUTMEG, TO GARNISH

◆ Preheat the slow cooker on HIGH while preparing ingredients. Heat oil in a large saucepan, add parsnips, potato and onion and sauté for 5 minutes.

◆ Add stock and seasoning and bring to the boil. Transfer to the cooking pot, cover, reduce temperature to LOW and cook for 6-8 hours, or until vegetables are cooked and tender.

◆ Cool slightly, then purée soup in a blender or food processor. Return soup to the rinsed-out cooking pot and stir in yogurt and nutmeg. Cover and cook on LOW for 30-60 minutes, or until heated through.

◆ Pour into warmed bowls, swirl in a little yogurt, sprinkle with nutmeg and serve.

Fresh Mushroom Soup

SERVES 4

*15G (¹/₂OZ) DRIED PORCINI
MUSHROOMS*

25G (1OZ) BUTTER

1 ONION, FINELY CHOPPED

*350G (12OZ) MUSHROOMS,
THINLY SLICED*

*750ML (27FL OZ)
VEGETABLE STOCK*

SALT AND GROUND BLACK PEPPER

150ML (5FL OZ) SINGLE CREAM

*2 TABLESPOONS CHOPPED
FRESH FLAT-LEAF PARSLEY*

◆ Preheat the slow cooker on HIGH while preparing ingredients. Place dried mushrooms in a small bowl, pour over 115ml (4fl oz) boiling water and leave to soak for 20 minutes.

◆ Drain mushrooms, reserving soaking liquid, then snip mushrooms into small pieces using scissors. Set aside.

◆ Melt butter in a pan, add onion and sauté for 3 minutes. Add mushrooms and soaked dried mushrooms and cook gently for 5 minutes, stirring occasionally. Stir in stock, reserved mushroom liquid and seasoning, then bring to the boil.

◆ Transfer to the cooking pot, cover, reduce the temperature to LOW and cook for 5 hours.

◆ Stir in cream, cover and cook on LOW for a further 30-60 minutes, or until hot.

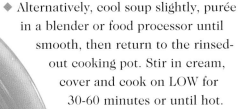

◆ Alternatively, cool soup slightly, purée in a blender or food processor until smooth, then return to the rinsed-out cooking pot. Stir in cream, cover and cook on LOW for 30-60 minutes or until hot.

◆ Stir in chopped parsley and serve with warm Italian bread, if desired.

Potato, Leek and Tomato Soup

SERVES 4

225G (8OZ) LEEKS, WHITE PART ONLY, THINLY SLICED

350G (12OZ) POTATOES, PEELED AND DICED

25G (1OZ) BUTTER

225G (8OZ) WELL-FLAVOURED TOMATOES, CHOPPED

SALT AND GROUND BLACK PEPPER

SINGLE CREAM, TO TASTE

FINELY CHOPPED FRESH CHERVIL OR PARSLEY, TO GARNISH

◆ Preheat the slow cooker on HIGH while preparing ingredients. Sauté leeks and potatoes in melted butter in a saucepan for 5 minutes.

◆ Add tomatoes and continue to cook until they start to give up their juices, then add 750ml (27fl oz) water and seasoning.

◆ Bring to the boil, then transfer to the cooking pot. Cover, reduce temperature to LOW and cook for 6-8 hours, or until potatoes are cooked and tender.

◆ Cool slightly, then pass soup through a vegetable mill, or purée it very briefly in a blender and press through a sieve.

◆ Return soup to the rinsed-out cooking pot, cover and cook on LOW for 30-60 minutes or until hot, adding a little cream to taste and adjusting consistency with extra boiling water, if necessary.

◆ Serve garnished with a fine sprinkling of chopped chervil or parsley. Serve with fresh crusty bread, if desired.

Spiced Vichyssoise

SERVES 4

55G (2OZ) BUTTER

4 LEEKS, FINELY CHOPPED

1 ONION, FINELY CHOPPED

2-3 TEASPOONS MILD CURRY PASTE

350G (12OZ) POTATOES, DICED

1 LITRE (1¾ PINTS) CHICKEN OR VEGETABLE STOCK

SALT AND GROUND BLACK PEPPER

150-175ML (5-6FL OZ) SINGLE CREAM

FRESH CORIANDER, TO GARNISH

◆ Preheat the slow cooker on HIGH while preparing ingredients. Melt butter in a saucepan and sauté leeks and onion for 5 minutes until softened. Stir in curry paste and potatoes and sauté for 2-3 minutes, then add stock and seasoning and bring to the boil.

◆ Transfer to the cooking pot, cover, reduce temperature to LOW and cook for 6-8 hours, or until vegetables are completely soft.

◆ Leave to cool slightly, then purée briefly in a blender (potatoes quickly turn 'gluey'). Adjust level of curry paste and seasoning if necessary.

◆ Stir in cream, cover and chill. Garnish with coriander and serve with fresh bread rolls, if desired.

Thai-Spiced Chicken Soup

SERVES 4-6

2 TABLESPOONS SUNFLOWER OIL

6 SHALLOTS, FINELY CHOPPED

450G (1LB) CARROTS,
THINLY SLICED

4 STICKS CELERY, THINLY SLICED

1 GARLIC CLOVE, CRUSHED

1 RED CHILLI, SEEDED
AND FINELY CHOPPED

2.5CM (1IN) PIECE FRESH GINGER,
PEELED AND FINELY CHOPPED

500G (1LB 2OZ) SKINLESS
BONELESS CHICKEN THIGHS, DICED

1 TABLESPOON
THAI 7-SPICE SEASONING

115G (4OZ) GREEN BEANS, SLICED

950ML (30FL OZ) CHICKEN STOCK

SALT AND GROUND BLACK PEPPER

85G (3OZ) SPAGHETTI,
BROKEN INTO SMALL LENGTHS

2-3 TABLESPOONS CHOPPED
FRESH CORIANDER

◆ Preheat the slow cooker on HIGH while preparing ingredients.

◆ Heat oil in a pan, add shallots, carrots, celery, garlic, chilli and ginger and sauté for 3 minutes. Add chicken and cook until sealed all over, stirring frequently.

◆ Add Thai spice and green beans and cook for 1 minute, stirring. Add stock and seasoning and bring to the boil. Transfer to the cooking pot, cover, then reduce temperature to LOW and cook for 5 hours.

◆ Stir in spaghetti, cover and cook on LOW for a further 1-2 hours or until spaghetti is cooked and tender.

◆ Stir in the chopped coriander and serve with fresh crusty bread, if desired.

Bacon and Sweetcorn Chowder

SERVES 4-6

25G (1OZ) BUTTER

225G (8OZ) LEAN SMOKED BACK
BACON RASHERS, DICED

1 LARGE ONION, CHOPPED

3 STICKS CELERY, FINELY CHOPPED

350G (12OZ) PEELED POTATOES,
FINELY DICED

175G (6OZ) BUTTON MUSHROOMS,
SLICED

950ML (30FL OZ)
VEGETABLE STOCK

SALT AND GROUND BLACK PEPPER

340G (12OZ) CAN SWEETCORN
KERNELS, DRAINED

4-6 TABLESPOONS SINGLE CREAM

3-4 TABLESPOONS CHOPPED
FRESH PARSLEY

Variation
Thicken soup with a little cornflour, if desired: blend 1-2 tablespoons cornflour with a little water and stir into soup. Cook on HIGH for 20-30 minutes.

◆ Preheat the slow cooker on HIGH while preparing ingredients. Melt butter in a pan, add bacon and cook for 3 minutes, stirring.

◆ Add onion, celery and potatoes and sauté for 5 minutes. Add mushrooms, stock and seasoning and stir to mix. Bring to the boil.

◆ Transfer soup to the cooking pot. Cover, reduce temperature to LOW and cook for 6 hours.

◆ Stir in sweetcorn, cover and cook on LOW for a further 1-2 hours. Stir in cream and chopped parsley and adjust seasoning to taste.

◆ Ladle into warmed soup bowls and serve with warm crusty bread or cornmeal bread, if desired.

Creamy Watercress Soup

SERVES 4

25G (1OZ) BUTTER

6 SHALLOTS, FINELY CHOPPED

1 LEEK, THINLY SLICED

*225G (8OZ) POTATOES,
PEELED AND DICED*

*225G (8OZ) WATERCRESS,
ROUGHLY CHOPPED*

*750ML (27FL OZ)
VEGETABLE STOCK*

SALT AND GROUND BLACK PEPPER

150ML (5FL OZ) SINGLE CREAM

◆ Preheat the slow cooker on HIGH while preparing ingredients.

◆ Melt butter in a pan, add shallots and leek and sauté for 5 minutes. Add potatoes and watercress and cook for 3 minutes or until watercress wilts, stirring occasionally.

◆ Add stock and seasoning, then bring to the boil. Transfer to the cooking pot, cover, reduce temperature to LOW and cook for 6-7 hours.

◆ Cool slightly, then purée mixture in a blender or food processor until smooth. Return soup to the rinsed-out cooking pot and stir in cream. Cover and cook on LOW for 30-60 minutes, or until hot.

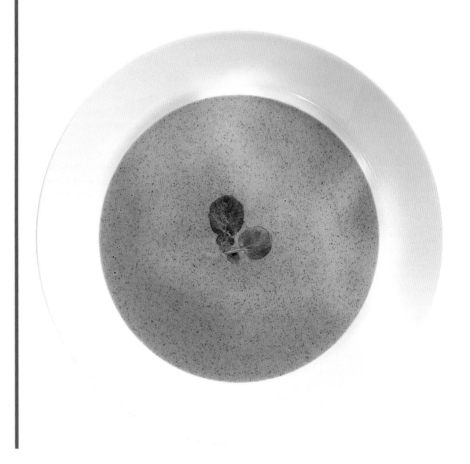

Mexican Bean Soup

SERVES 4-6

225G (8OZ) DRIED RED KIDNEY
BEANS, SOAKED OVERNIGHT

2 TABLESPOONS OLIVE OIL

2 RED ONIONS, FINELY CHOPPED

2 GARLIC CLOVES, CRUSHED

1 RED PEPPER, SEEDED AND DICED

1 FRESH RED CHILLI, SEEDED
AND FINELY CHOPPED

2 TEASPOONS GROUND CORIANDER

1 TEASPOON GROUND CUMIN

400G (14OZ) CAN
CHOPPED TOMATOES

950ML (30FL OZ)
VEGETABLE STOCK

3 TEASPOONS CHILLI SAUCE,
PLUS EXTRA TO TASTE

SALT AND GROUND BLACK PEPPER

2-3 TABLESPOONS CHOPPED
FRESH CORIANDER

4 TABLESPOONS CRÈME FRAÎCHE
(OPTIONAL)

Variation
Once cooked, cool soup slightly,
purée in a blender or food processor
until smooth, then reheat on LOW for
30-60 minutes or until hot.

◆ Preheat slow cooker on HIGH while preparing ingredients. Drain kidney beans, place in a large pan, cover with cold water and bring to the boil. Boil rapidly for 10 minutes, then rinse, drain and set aside.

◆ Meanwhile, heat oil in a large pan, add onions, garlic, pepper and chilli and sauté for 5 minutes. Add ground coriander and cumin and cook gently for 1 minute, stirring.

◆ Add kidney beans, tomatoes, stock, chilli sauce and seasoning and bring to the boil. Transfer to the cooking pot, cover, reduce temperature to LOW and cook for 8-12 hours.

◆ Stir in chopped coriander and extra chilli sauce, if desired. Stir in crème fraîche, if using, and ladle into warmed soup bowls.

Plum Tomato Soup

SERVES 6

1KG (2¼LB) PLUM TOMATOES

2 TABLESPOONS OLIVE OIL

1 LARGE RED ONION, THINLY SLICED

2 GARLIC CLOVES, CRUSHED

1 RED PEPPER, PEELED, SEEDED
AND THINLY SLICED

2 TABLESPOONS
SUN-DRIED TOMATO PASTE

2 TEASPOONS CASTER SUGAR

950ML (30FL OZ) VEGETABLE STOCK

SALT AND GROUND BLACK PEPPER

FRESH PARMESAN SHAVINGS,
TO SERVE (OPTIONAL)

◆ Preheat the slow cooker on HIGH while preparing ingredients. Using a sharp knife, cut a small cross in the base of each tomato. Place tomatoes in a bowl, cover with boiling water and leave for 30 seconds. Using a slotted spoon, remove and plunge into cold water, then drain well. Peel off and discard skins, then chop flesh and set aside.

◆ Heat oil in a large pan, add onion, garlic and red pepper and sauté for 5 minutes. Stir in tomatoes, sun-dried tomato paste, sugar, stock and seasoning, then bring to the boil.

◆ Transfer to cooking pot and cover. Switch setting to AUTO and cook for 8-10 hours.

◆ Cool soup slightly, then purée mixture in a blender or food processor until smooth. Return soup to cooking pot, cover and cook on LOW for 30-60 minutes, or until hot. Sprinkle Parmesan shavings over soup to serve, if desired.

Celeriac and Dill Soup

SERVES 4-6

55G (2OZ) BUTTER

1 BAY LEAF

2 TABLESPOONS CHOPPED
FRESH DILL

1 ONION, FINELY CHOPPED

1 MEDIUM CELERIAC,
WEIGHING ABOUT 575G (1¼LB),
CUT INTO SMALL CUBES

950ML (30FL OZ) GOOD, STRONG
VEGETABLE STOCK

SALT AND GROUND BLACK PEPPER

3 TABLESPOONS SINGLE CREAM

2 TEASPOONS LEMON JUICE

◆ Preheat the slow cooker on HIGH while preparing ingredients. Melt butter in a saucepan with bay leaf and 1 tablespoon dill. Simmer over a gentle heat for 1-2 minutes to allow flavours to develop.

◆ Add onion and celeriac, cover and simmer gently for about 10 minutes until softened. Add stock and seasoning and bring to boil.

◆ Transfer to the cooking pot, cover, reduce temperature to LOW and cook for 6-8 hours, or until vegetables are tender. Remove bay leaf.

◆ Cool slightly, then purée soup in a blender or food processor until smooth. Return to the rinsed-out cooking pot, cover and cook on LOW for 30-60 minutes, or until hot.

◆ Stir in cream, lemon juice and remaining dill. Check seasoning, adjusting if necessary, and serve with warm crusty bread, if desired.

Farmhouse Paté

6 THIN SLICES PARMA HAM

25G (1OZ) BUTTER

1 ONION, FINELY CHOPPED

1 GARLIC CLOVE, CRUSHED

115G (4OZ) MUSHROOMS, CHOPPED

225G (8OZ) CHICKEN LIVERS,
TRIMMED AND DICED

225G (8OZ) SKINLESS BONELESS
CHICKEN BREAST, DICED

225G (8OZ) MINCED PORK

115G (4OZ) STREAKY BACON, DICED

2 TABLESPOONS BRANDY

2 TABLESPOONS GREEN
PEPPERCORNS IN BRINE, DRAINED

4 TEASPOONS CHOPPED
FRESH THYME

SALT AND GROUND BLACK PEPPER

FRESH HERB SPRIGS, TO GARNISH

CRUSTY FRENCH BREAD,
TO SERVE

◆ Line the base and sides of 1.2-litre (2-pint) ovenproof dish with Parma ham, allowing edges to hang over sides of dish. Set aside.

◆ Melt butter in a pan, add onion, garlic and mushrooms and sauté for 5 minutes. Add chicken livers, chicken breast, pork and bacon and cook until meat is coloured all over, stirring frequently. Cool slightly.

◆ Mince in a blender or food processor with brandy. Transfer to a bowl and stir in peppercorns, chopped thyme and seasoning. Mix well. Spoon into prepared dish and press down lightly, levelling the surface.

◆ Fold Parma ham over the top, then cover with aluminium foil. Place in the cooking pot of the slow cooker. Add sufficient boiling water to the cooking pot to come halfway up the sides of the dish.

◆ Cover and cook on HIGH for 5-6 hours or until cooked and the juices of the paté run clear when pierced with a skewer.

◆ Lift out, remove foil, drain off any excess juices and leave to cool. Chill before serving.

◆ Turn out onto a serving plate and garnish with fresh herb sprigs. Serve with crusty French bread.

Chicken Liver Paté

SERVES 6-8

6 RASHERS RINDLESS
STREAKY BACON

40G (1½OZ) BUTTER

1 ONION, FINELY CHOPPED

2 GARLIC CLOVES, CRUSHED

450G (1LB) CHICKEN LIVERS,
TRIMMED AND HALVED

2 TABLESPOONS RUBY PORT

2 TABLESPOONS DOUBLE CREAM

1½ TEASPOONS
DRIED MIXED HERBS

SALT AND GROUND BLACK PEPPER

MIXED SALAD LEAVES, TO GARNISH

TOAST OR WARM CRUSTY BREAD,
TO SERVE

◆ Stretch bacon rashers using the back of a knife. Line the base and sides of a 15cm (6in) round ovenproof dish with the bacon. Set aside.

◆ Melt butter in a pan, add onion and garlic and cook gently for 5 minutes, stirring occasionally. Add chicken livers and cook for about 5 minutes or until sealed all over, stirring occasionally.

◆ Remove pan from the heat, cool slightly, then stir in port, cream, dried herbs and seasoning. Purée mixture in a blender or food processor until smooth. Spoon into the prepared dish and level the surface. Cover with aluminium foil.

◆ Place in the cooking pot of the slow cooker and add sufficient boiling water to the cooking pot to come halfway up the sides of the dish. Cover and cook on HIGH for 5-6 hours or until thoroughly cooked. Lift out, remove foil and leave to cool. Chill before serving.

◆ Turn out onto a serving plate and garnish with salad leaves. Serve with toast or warm crusty bread.

Aubergine Dip

SERVES 6-8

900G (2LB) AUBERGINES

4 TABLESPOONS OLIVE OIL

6 SHALLOTS, FINELY CHOPPED

2 GARLIC CLOVES, CRUSHED

*225G (8OZ) LARGE FLAT
(FIELD) MUSHROOMS, CHOPPED*

*1½ TEASPOONS
GROUND CORIANDER*

1½ TEASPOONS GROUND CUMIN

4 TABLESPOONS DRY WHITE WINE

SALT AND GROUND BLACK PEPPER

*4 TABLESPOONS CHOPPED
FRESH CORIANDER*

*BREADSTICKS, VEGETABLE
CRUDITÉS OR TOASTED ITALIAN
BREAD, TO SERVE*

◆ Trim and dice aubergines. Set aside. Heat oil in a large pan, add shallots and garlic and sauté for 3 minutes. Add aubergines and mushrooms and cook for 10-15 minutes or until soft, stirring occasionally.

◆ Add coriander and cumin and cook for 1 minute, stirring. Remove pan from the heat and cool slightly.

◆ Place mixture in a blender or food processor with wine and seasoning and blend until smooth and well mixed.

◆ Transfer mixture to the cooking pot in the slow cooker and level the surface. Cover and cook on LOW for 4-5 hours.

◆ Stir in chopped coriander and serve with breadsticks, vegetable crudités or toasted Italian bread.

Variation
Cool and chill before serving. If serving cold, stir 4-6 tablespoons crème fraîche into the dip just before serving, if desired.

Fish

Rosemary-Baked Mackerel

◆ Preheat the slow cooker on HIGH while preparing ingredients. Place onion, apple, tomatoes and stock in a saucepan. Add rosemary and Worcestershire sauce and season with salt and pepper. Bring to a boil, then cover and simmer for 5 minutes.

◆ Fold mackerel fillets in half with skin side outermost and place in the cooking pot. Pour sauce over fish.

◆ Cover, reduce temperature to LOW and cook for 2-3 hours, or until fish is cooked.

Mackerel with Sour Cream

SERVES 4

25G (1OZ) BUTTER

1 LEEK, THINLY SLICED

227G (8OZ) CAN
CHOPPED TOMATOES

2 TABLESPOONS VEGETABLE STOCK
OR DRY WHITE WINE

1 TABLESPOON CHOPPED FRESH DILL

½ TEASPOON MILD PAPRIKA

JUICE ½ LEMON

SALT AND GROUND BLACK PEPPER

4 MACKEREL FILLETS,
EACH WEIGHING ABOUT 115G (4OZ)

150ML (5FL OZ) THICK SOUR CREAM

DILL SPRIGS, TO GARNISH

◆ Preheat the slow cooker on HIGH while preparing ingredients. Melt butter in a saucepan, add leek and sauté for 5 minutes. Add tomatoes, stock or wine, chopped dill, paprika, lemon juice and seasoning and bring to the boil.

◆ Place mackerel fillets in the cooking pot, skin side down. Pour leek and tomato sauce over fish. Cover, reduce temperature to LOW and cook for 3-4 hours, or until fish is cooked.

◆ Drizzle over sour cream, garnish with dill sprigs and serve. Serve with cooked fresh vegetables, such as mangetout, if desired.

Fish Couscous

900G (2LB) WHITE FISH FILLETS,
SKINNED AND CUT INTO
SMALL CHUNKS

3 TABLESPOONS OLIVE OIL

1 LARGE ONION, FINELY CHOPPED

2 GARLIC CLOVES, CHOPPED

1 TABLESPOON CHOPPED
FRESH THYME

2 CARROTS, FINELY CHOPPED

115G (4OZ) BUTTON MUSHROOMS

300ML (10FL OZ) PASSATA

400G (14OZ) CAN CHICKPEAS,
DRAINED

55G (2OZ) RAISINS

55G (2OZ) CASHEW NUTS, TOASTED

350G (12OZ) COUSCOUS

2 TABLESPOONS CHOPPED
FRESH PARSLEY

SALT AND GROUND BLACK PEPPER

SPICE MIX

1 TABLESPOON CORIANDER SEEDS,
TOASTED

1 TABLESPOON CUMIN SEEDS,
TOASTED

2 TEASPOONS CINNAMON

2 TEASPOONS TURMERIC

GRATED ZEST AND JUICE ½ LEMON

2 TEASPOONS HARISSA PASTE

3 TABLESPOONS EXTRA VIRGIN
OLIVE OIL

◆ To make spice mix, using a pestle and mortar, combine toasted coriander and cumin seeds, cinnamon, turmeric, lemon zest and juice, harissa paste and olive oil and grind to make a smooth paste.

◆ Wash and dry fish and place in a non-metallic dish. Add 2 tablespoons of spice mix and turn fish to coat thoroughly. Cover dish and place in the refrigerator to marinate for several hours, or overnight if possible.

◆ Preheat the slow cooker on HIGH while preparing ingredients. Heat oil in a large saucepan and sauté onion, garlic, thyme, carrots and mushrooms for 10 minutes, or until softened. Add 1 tablespoon spice mix and sauté for a further 1 minute. Stir in passata and chickpeas and bring to the boil.

◆ Stir in raisins, cashew nuts and marinated fish. Transfer to cooking pot, cover, reduce temperature to LOW and cook for 2-4 hours, or until fish and vegetables are cooked and tender.

◆ Meanwhile, wash couscous with cold water and spread out over a large baking sheet. Pour over 450ml (16fl oz) water and leave to soak for 20 minutes.

◆ Steam couscous, either in a double boiler, or in a muslin-lined steamer for 8-10 minutes until fluffed up and tender.

◆ Sprinkle parsley over fish stew and season to taste. Spoon couscous onto a serving plate and top with fish stew. Serve.

Tuna, Tomato and Olive Casserole

SERVES 6

2 TABLESPOONS OLIVE OIL

1 RED ONION, THINLY SLICED

1 YELLOW PEPPER, SEEDED
AND THINLY SLICED

2 GARLIC CLOVES, CRUSHED

2 TABLESPOONS PLAIN FLOUR

200ML (7FL OZ) FISH
OR VEGETABLE STOCK

150ML (5FL OZ) RED
OR DRY WHITE WINE

700G (1½LB) PLUM TOMATOES,
PEELED AND CHOPPED

225G (8OZ) BUTTON MUSHROOMS,
HALVED

2 COURGETTES, SLICED

SALT AND GROUND BLACK PEPPER

400G (14OZ) CAN TUNA IN BRINE
OR SPRING WATER

340G (12OZ) CAN SWEETCORN
KERNELS, DRAINED

85G (3OZ) PITTED BLACK OLIVES

2 TABLESPOONS CHOPPED
FRESH MIXED HERBS

COOKED PASTA, TO SERVE

Variations
Use canned salmon in place of tuna.
Use 400g (14oz) can chickpeas,
rinsed and drained, in place of
sweetcorn.

◆ Preheat slow cooker on HIGH while preparing ingredients. Heat oil in a pan, add onion, pepper and garlic and sauté for 5 minutes.

◆ Stir in flour and cook for 1 minute, stirring. Gradually stir in stock and wine, then add tomatoes, mushrooms, courgettes and seasoning and bring to the boil, stirring.

◆ Transfer to the cooking pot, cover and cook on HIGH for 3-4 hours.

◆ Drain and flake tuna. Stir tuna, sweetcorn and olives into vegetable sauce. Cover and cook on HIGH for a further 1-2 hours, or until casserole is piping hot.

◆ Stir in chopped fresh mixed herbs and serve with cooked pasta, such as fusilli or penne.

Salmon and Broccoli Risotto

◆ Preheat the slow cooker on HIGH while preparing ingredients. Melt butter in a pan, add shallots, garlic, pepper and mushrooms and sauté for 5 minutes.

◆ Add rice and cook for 1 minute, stirring. Stir in wine, 450ml (16fl oz) stock and seasoning and bring to the boil.

◆ Transfer to the cooking pot, cover and cook on HIGH for 1-2 hours or until rice is just tender and most of the liquid has been absorbed.

◆ Meanwhile, cook broccoli in a pan of boiling water for about 5 minutes or until just tender. Drain well.

◆ Stir broccoli and salmon into risotto, adding a little extra hot stock if required. Cover and cook on HIGH for about 30 minutes.

◆ Stir in chopped parsley, serve in individual dishes and sprinkle with Parmesan shavings.

Variation
Use 400g (14oz) can pink or red salmon, drained, boned and flaked, in place of cooked fresh salmon.

Sicilian Salt Cod

900G (2LB) SALT COD

MILK

4 TABLESPOONS SEASONED
PLAIN FLOUR

4 TABLESPOONS OLIVE OIL

225G (8OZ) BABY ONIONS, HALVED

2 GARLIC CLOVES, CHOPPED

4 RIPE TOMATOES, CHOPPED

115G (4OZ) SULTANAS

55G (2OZ) PITTED BLACK OLIVES,
HALVED

2 TABLESPOONS BALSAMIC VINEGAR

150ML (5FL OZ) CHICKEN
OR VEGETABLE STOCK

2 TABLESPOONS TOMATO PURÉE

1 TEASPOON SUGAR

PEPPER

2 TABLESPOONS CHOPPED
FRESH PARSLEY

◆ Wash salt cod, place in a bowl and cover with cold water. Leave to soak for 12 hours, changing water several times if possible.

◆ Drain fish, rinse under cold running water and pat dry. Remove skin and cut the flesh into small chunks. Place in a shallow dish, cover with milk and leave to soak for a further 2 hours. Wash fish again, pat dry and dust lightly in seasoned flour.

◆ Preheat the slow cooker on HIGH. Heat half the oil in a non-stick frying pan. Add cod and cook for 3 minutes until sealed all over. Remove with a slotted spoon and set aside.

◆ Add remaining oil to the pan and sauté onions and garlic for about 5 minutes or until softened. Add tomatoes, sultanas, olives, vinegar, stock, tomato purée, sugar and pepper. Bring to the boil, then stir in cod. Transfer to the cooking pot, cover, reduce temperature to LOW and cook for 2-4 hours, or until fish and vegetables are cooked.

◆ Sprinkle with parsley and serve with rice, pasta or bread, if desired.

Poultry
and Game

Italian Chicken Cassoulet

SERVES 6

*175G (6OZ) DRIED BLACK-EYE
OR BORLOTTI BEANS,
SOAKED OVERNIGHT*

2 TABLESPOONS OLIVE OIL

4 CHICKEN PORTIONS, SKINNED

*2 LARGE RED ONIONS,
THINLY SLICED*

2 GARLIC CLOVES, CRUSHED

2 RED PEPPERS, SEEDED AND DICED

2 TABLESPOONS PLAIN FLOUR

250ML (9FL OZ) CHICKEN STOCK

150ML (5FL OZ) RED WINE

*400G (14OZ) CAN
CHOPPED TOMATOES*

225G (8OZ) MUSHROOMS, SLICED

*1 TABLESPOON CHOPPED
FRESH THYME*

*1 TABLESPOON CHOPPED
FRESH OREGANO*

*SALT AND GROUND
BLACK PEPPER*

*FRESH HERB SPRIGS,
TO GARNISH*

◆ Preheat the slow cooker on HIGH while preparing ingredients. Drain beans, place in a large pan, cover with fresh cold water and bring to the boil. Boil for 10 minutes, then rinse, drain and set aside.

◆ Meanwhile, heat oil in a large pan, add chicken portions and cook until lightly browned all over, turning occasionally. Transfer to the cooking pot and set aside.

◆ Add onions, garlic and peppers to the pan and sauté for 5 minutes. Stir in flour and cook for 1 minute, stirring. Gradually stir in stock and wine, then add beans, tomatoes, mushrooms, herbs and seasoning.

◆ Bring to the boil, stirring, then pour over chicken in the cooking pot. Cover and cook on HIGH for 2 hours.

◆ Reduce temperature to LOW and cook for a further 4-6 hours, or until chicken is cooked and tender.

◆ Garnish chicken with fresh herb sprigs and serve with warm ciabatta bread and a mixed green salad, if desired.

Fragrant Chicken Curry

3 TABLESPOONS SUNFLOWER OIL

2 ONIONS, CHOPPED

4 CARROTS, THINLY SLICED

2 GARLIC CLOVES, CRUSHED

*1 FRESH GREEN CHILLI, SEEDED AND
FINELY CHOPPED*

*2.5CM (1IN) PIECE FRESH GINGER,
PEELED AND FINELY CHOPPED*

2 TABLESPOONS PLAIN FLOUR

2 TEASPOONS TURMERIC

2 TEASPOONS GROUND CORIANDER

2 TEASPOONS GROUND CUMIN

SALT AND GROUND BLACK PEPPER

*700G (1½LB) SKINLESS BONELESS
CHICKEN THIGHS, DICED*

300ML (10FL OZ) CHICKEN STOCK

150ML (5FL OZ) PASSATA

115G (4OZ) SULTANAS

*55G (2OZ)
TOASTED CASHEW NUTS*

*2-3 TABLESPOONS
CHOPPED FRESH
CORIANDER*

◆ Preheat the slow cooker on HIGH while preparing ingredients. Heat 1 tablespoon oil in a pan, add onions, carrots, garlic, chilli and ginger and sauté for 5 minutes. Transfer to the cooking pot and set aside.

◆ In a small bowl, combine flour, turmeric, coriander, cumin and salt and pepper. Toss chicken in spiced flour until coated all over.

◆ Heat remaining oil in the pan, add chicken in batches and cook quickly until sealed all over. Transfer to the cooking pot.

◆ Add stock and passata to pan and bring to boil, stirring and scraping up sediments in the pan. Add to the cooking pot and stir to mix well. Cover cooking pot, reduce temperature to LOW and cook for 6 hours.

◆ Stir in sultanas, cover and cook on LOW for a further 1-2 hours, or until chicken is cooked and tender.

◆ Stir in cashew nuts and chopped coriander. Serve with plain boiled rice and a mixed leaf salad, if desired.

Chicken Tagine with Figs, Olives and Pistachio Nuts

SERVES 4

2 TABLESPOONS OLIVE OIL

8 CHICKEN THIGHS, SKINNED

2 ONIONS, CHOPPED

2 CARROTS, THINLY SLICED

2 GARLIC CLOVES, CRUSHED

2 TEASPOONS GRATED
FRESH GINGER

175G (6OZ) BUTTON MUSHROOMS,
HALVED

8 LARGE DRIED FIGS,
ROUGHLY CHOPPED

2 TABLESPOONS PLAIN FLOUR

400ML (14FL OZ) CHICKEN STOCK

2 TABLESPOONS TOMATO PURÉE

1 TABLESPOON LEMON JUICE

85G (3OZ) BLACK OLIVES

40G (1½OZ) PISTACHIO NUTS
OR PINE NUTS

CHOPPED FRESH PARSLEY,
TO GARNISH

SPICE MIX

2 TABLESPOONS OLIVE OIL

2 TEASPOONS GROUND CORIANDER

2 TEASPOONS GROUND CUMIN

1½ TEASPOONS GROUND CINNAMON

1½ TEASPOONS TURMERIC

FINELY GRATED ZEST AND
JUICE ½ LEMON

1½ TEASPOONS HARISSA PASTE

◆ To make spice mix, combine olive oil, coriander, cumin, cinnamon, turmeric, lemon zest and juice and harissa paste in a small bowl. Toss chicken thighs in spice mix until coated all over.

◆ Preheat the slow cooker on HIGH. Heat oil in a pan, add chicken and cook until lightly browned all over, turning occasionally. Transfer to the cooking pot using a slotted spoon. Set aside.

◆ Add onions, carrots, garlic and ginger to the pan and sauté for about 5 minutes, or until slightly softened.

◆ Add mushrooms and figs, then stir in flour and cook for 1 minute, stirring. Gradually stir in stock, then add tomato purée and lemon juice. Bring slowly to the boil, stirring, then pour over chicken in the cooking pot. Stir gently to mix.

◆ Cover cooking pot and cook chicken on HIGH for 3-5 hours until cooked and tender.

◆ About 1 hour before serving, stir olives and nuts into chicken. Serve garnished with parsley and with couscous or rice.

Chicken Cacciatore

SERVES 4

2 TABLESPOONS OLIVE OIL

*4 SKINLESS CHICKEN BREASTS,
WITH BONES*

1 RED ONION, THINLY SLICED

2 GARLIC CLOVES, THINLY SLICED

1 RED PEPPER, SEEDED AND SLICED

*1 YELLOW PEPPER,
SEEDED AND SLICED*

2 TABLESPOONS PLAIN FLOUR

150ML (5FL OZ) RED WINE

150ML (5FL OZ) CHICKEN STOCK

*400G (14OZ) CAN
CHOPPED TOMATOES*

1 TABLESPOON TOMATO PURÉE

SALT AND GROUND BLACK PEPPER

PINCH SUGAR

*2 TABLESPOONS CHOPPED
FRESH BASIL*

◆ Preheat the slow cooker on HIGH while preparing ingredients. In a pan, heat oil and fry chicken breasts all over until golden brown, then transfer to the cooking pot using a slotted spoon.

◆ Gently sauté onion, garlic and peppers in pan for 5 minutes without browning. Stir in flour and cook for 1 minute, stirring.

◆ Add wine, stock, tomatoes, tomato purée, salt and pepper and sugar and bring to the boil.

◆ Pour over chicken in cooking pot, cover and cook on HIGH for 3-5 hours, or until chicken is cooked and tender.

◆ Serve on a bed of pasta noodles, if desired, and sprinkle with basil and plenty of black pepper.

Coq au Vin

25G (1OZ) BUTTER

4 CHICKEN JOINTS, SKINNED

350G (12OZ) SHALLOTS
OR BUTTON ONIONS

2 GARLIC CLOVES, CRUSHED

350G (12OZ) CARROTS,
THINLY SLICED

175G (6OZ) LEAN SMOKED
BACK BACON, DICED

25G (1OZ) PLAIN FLOUR

225ML (8FL OZ) CHICKEN STOCK

200ML (7FL OZ) RED WINE

2 TABLESPOONS TOMATO PURÉE

225G (8OZ) BUTTON MUSHROOMS

SALT AND GROUND BLACK PEPPER

1 BOUQUET GARNI

FRESH HERB SPRIGS, TO GARNISH

◆ Preheat the slow cooker on HIGH while preparing ingredients. Melt butter in a pan. Add chicken portions and cook until lightly browned all over, turning occasionally. Transfer to the cooking pot using a slotted spoon and set aside.

◆ Add shallots or button onions, garlic, carrots and bacon and sauté for 5 minutes. Stir in flour and cook for 1 minute, stirring. Gradually stir in stock and wine, then bring to the boil, stirring.

◆ Add tomato purée, mushrooms, seasoning and bouquet garni and pour over chicken in cooking pot. Cover and cook on HIGH for 3-5 hours, or until chicken is cooked and tender.

◆ Remove and discard bouquet garni. Garnish chicken with fresh herb sprigs. Serve with plain boiled rice or with boiled egg noodles tossed in melted butter, if desired.

Chicken with Shallots

SERVES 4

1 TABLESPOON OLIVE OIL

25G (1OZ) BUTTER

4 CHICKEN PORTIONS, SKINNED

450G (1LB) SHALLOTS, HALVED

2 GARLIC CLOVES, THINLY SLICED

*175G (6OZ) LEAN SMOKED OR
UNSMOKED BACK BACON, DICED*

2 TABLESPOONS PLAIN FLOUR

*225ML (8FL OZ) DRY WHITE
OR ROSÉ WINE*

200ML (7FL OZ) CHICKEN STOCK

175G (6OZ) BUTTON MUSHROOMS

*1 TABLESPOON WHOLEGRAIN
MUSTARD*

2 BAY LEAVES

SALT AND GROUND BLACK PEPPER

*2 TABLESPOONS CHOPPED
FRESH FLAT-LEAF PARSLEY*

Variations
*Use button onions in place of
shallots. Use Dijon mustard in place
of wholegrain mustard.*

◆ Preheat the slow cooker on HIGH while preparing ingredients. Heat oil and butter in a pan, add chicken and cook until lightly browned all over. Transfer to the cooking pot using a slotted spoon and set aside.

◆ Add shallots, garlic and bacon to the pan and sauté for 5 minutes. Stir in flour and cook for 1 minute, stirring. Gradually stir in wine and stock, then bring to the boil, stirring.

◆ Add mushrooms, mustard, bay leaves and seasoning, then pour over chicken in the cooking pot. Cover and cook on HIGH for 3-5 hours, or until chicken is cooked and tender.

◆ Remove and discard bay leaves. Sprinkle with parsley. Serve with mustard-flavoured mashed potatoes and green cabbage, if desired.

Moroccan Chicken Casserole

SERVES 4

1.5KG (3½LB) CHICKEN, CUT INTO 8 PIECES AND SKINNED

4 TABLESPOONS LEMON JUICE

5 TABLESPOONS VIRGIN OLIVE OIL

1 TABLESPOON FINELY CHOPPED GARLIC

1 TEASPOON GROUND GINGER

1 TEASPOON CUMIN

1 TEASPOON GROUND CORIANDER

1 TEASPOON CINNAMON

LARGE PINCH SAFFRON THREADS

½ TEASPOON GROUND BLACK PEPPER

1 ONION, THINLY SLICED

2 TABLESPOONS PLAIN FLOUR

450ML (16FL OZ) CHICKEN STOCK

175G (6OZ) PITTED READY-TO-EAT DRIED PRUNES

SMALL BUNCH CORIANDER LEAVES

◆ Place chicken pieces in a large non-metallic dish and sprinkle over lemon juice, 3 tablespoons oil and garlic. Marinate for 2-4 hours.

◆ Preheat the slow cooker on HIGH. Remove chicken from marinade using a slotted spoon and reserve marinade. Heat remaining oil in a large pan, add chicken portions and cook until lightly browned all over. Add ginger, cumin, coriander, cinnamon, saffron threads and pepper and cook for 1 minute. Transfer to cooking pot using a slotted spoon.

◆ Add onion to pan and sauté for 5 minutes, then add flour and cook for 1 minute, stirring. Stir in stock and reserved marinade, then bring to the boil, stirring. Pour over chicken.

◆ Cover and cook on HIGH for 3-5 hours or until chicken is cooked and tender. About 1 hour before serving, stir in prunes.

◆ Shred coriander leaves and scatter over casserole. Serve with steamed couscous, if desired.

Lemon-baked Chicken

SERVES 4

2 LEMONS

1.35KG (3LB) OVEN-READY CHICKEN

1 SMALL ONION, QUARTERED

2 TABLESPOONS OLIVE OIL

85G (3OZ) BUTTER

2 GARLIC CLOVES, THINLY SLICED

4 TABLESPOONS BRANDY

*2 TABLESPOONS CHOPPED
FRESH FLAT-LEAF PARSLEY*

*FRESH FLAT-LEAF PARSLEY SPRIGS,
TO GARNISH*

◆ Preheat the slow cooker on HIGH while preparing ingredients. Cut 1 lemon into quarters and push into cavity of chicken, together with onion quarters.

◆ Heat oil and butter in a frying pan and quickly brown chicken all over. Transfer chicken to cooking pot using a slotted spoon. Set aside.

◆ Grate zest of remaining lemon and add to the pan with garlic. Sauté for 3 minutes. Squeeze juice from lemon and add to pan with brandy and chopped parsley.

◆ Bring gently to the boil, stirring. Pour over chicken in the cooking pot, then cover and cook on HIGH for 4-6 hours, or until chicken is cooked and tender.

◆ Carve chicken and serve with juices spooned over. Garnish with parsley sprigs to serve.

Barbecued Chicken

SERVES 4

40G (1½OZ) BUTTER

8 CHICKEN DRUMSTICKS, SKINNED

2 RED ONIONS, THINLY SLICED

2 TABLESPOONS PLAIN FLOUR

275ML (9½FL OZ) CHICKEN STOCK

2 TABLESPOONS TOMATO PURÉE

4 TABLESPOONS RED WINE VINEGAR

4 TABLESPOONS WORCESTERSHIRE SAUCE

1 TABLESPOON MUSTARD POWDER

SALT AND GROUND BLACK PEPPER

FRESH HERB SPRIGS, TO GARNISH

◆ Preheat the slow cooker on HIGH while preparing ingredients. Melt butter in a pan, add chicken drumsticks and cook until lightly browned all over, turning occasionally. Transfer to the cooking pot using a slotted spoon and set aside.

◆ Add onions to pan and sauté gently for 10 minutes. Stir in flour and cook for 1 minute, stirring. Gradually stir in stock, then add tomato purée, vinegar, Worcestershire sauce, mustard powder and seasoning.

◆ Bring to the boil, stirring, then pour over chicken in the cooking pot. Cover and cook on HIGH for 3-5 hours, or until chicken is cooked and tender.

◆ Garnish with fresh herb sprigs and serve with roast baby new potatoes and a mixed green salad, if desired.

Chicken with Potatoes, Tomatoes and Fennel

SERVES 4

2 TABLESPOONS OLIVE OIL

4 CHICKEN DRUMSTICKS, SKINNED

4 CHICKEN THIGHS, SKINNED

*55G (2OZ) THICK-CUT BACON,
DICED*

*2 SMALL FENNEL BULBS,
CUT INTO WEDGES, FEATHERY
FRONDS RESERVED*

*450G (1LB) POTATOES, PEELED
AND THINLY SLICED*

*1 SMALL GARLIC CLOVE,
FINELY CHOPPED*

2 TABLESPOONS PLAIN FLOUR

*400ML (14FL OZ) CHICKEN STOCK,
OR 200ML (7FL OZ) EACH CHICKEN
STOCK AND DRY WHITE WINE*

*1½ TEASPOONS CHOPPED
FRESH THYME*

1 TEASPOON GRATED LEMON ZEST

SALT AND GROUND BLACK PEPPER

*225G (8OZ) WELL-FLAVOURED
RIPE TOMATOES, QUARTERED*

*2 TABLESPOONS CHOPPED
FRESH PARSLEY AND RESERVED
FENNEL FRONDS*

◆ Preheat the slow cooker on HIGH while preparing ingredients. Heat 1 tablespoon oil in a large pan, add chicken drumsticks and thighs and fry until lightly browned all over. Transfer to the cooking pot using a slotted spoon.

◆ Heat remaining oil in the pan, add bacon, fennel, potatoes and garlic and sauté for 5 minutes. Stir in flour and cook for 1 minute, stirring. Stir in stock, and wine if using, and bring to the boil, stirring.

◆ Pour over chicken in cooking pot, add thyme, lemon zest and seasoning and stir to mix. Tuck tomatoes around and between chicken pieces.

◆ Cover and cook on HIGH for 4-6 hours, or until chicken and vegetables are cooked and tender.

◆ Mix together parsley and fennel fronds and scatter over casserole to serve. Serve with mashed potatoes and fresh peas, if desired.

Country Chicken Casserole

SERVES 4-6

25G (1OZ) BUTTER

4 SKINLESS BONELESS CHICKEN BREASTS, EACH CUT INTO 3 PIECES

350G (12OZ) BUTTON ONIONS OR SHALLOTS

2 LEEKS, THINLY SLICED

2 STICKS CELERY, THINLY SLICED

225G (8OZ) BABY CARROTS

225G (8OZ) BUTTON MUSHROOMS

55G (2OZ) PEARL BARLEY

400G (14OZ) CAN CHOPPED TOMATOES

2 TABLESPOONS TOMATO PURÉE

250ML (9FL OZ) CHICKEN STOCK

250ML (9FL OZ) DRY WHITE WINE

SALT AND GROUND BLACK PEPPER

1 BOUQUET GARNI

FRESH HERB SPRIGS, TO GARNISH

◆ Preheat the slow cooker on HIGH while preparing ingredients. Melt butter in a pan, add chicken and cook until lightly browned all over, stirring occasionally. Transfer to the cooking pot using a slotted spoon and set aside.

◆ Add onions or shallots, leeks, celery, carrots and mushrooms and sauté for 5 minutes. Stir in pearl barley, tomatoes, tomato purée, stock, wine and seasoning, then bring to the boil.

◆ Add bouquet garni, then pour over chicken in the cooking pot. Cover, reduce the temperature to LOW and cook for 8-10 hours or until chicken is cooked and tender.

◆ Garnish with fresh herb sprigs and serve with mashed potatoes and French beans, if desired.

Variation
Use small turkey breast steaks in place of chicken breasts.

Poussins Braised in Wine

4 POUSSINS, EACH WEIGHING ABOUT 350G (12OZ)

1 LEMON, CUT INTO QUARTERS

FEW SPRIGS FRESH CORIANDER

40G (1½OZ) BUTTER

2 LEEKS, SLICED

150ML (5FL OZ) RED WINE

2 TABLESPOONS CLEAR HONEY

SALT AND GROUND BLACK PEPPER

1 TABLESPOON CORNFLOUR

FRESH CORIANDER SPRIGS, TO GARNISH

◆ Preheat the slow cooker on HIGH while preparing ingredients. Stuff each poussin with one quarter of lemon and 1-2 sprigs of coriander.

◆ Melt butter in a frying pan and quickly brown birds all over. Transfer them to the cooking pot, using a slotted spoon. Set aside.

◆ Add leeks to pan and sauté for 5 minutes. Add wine, honey and seasoning and bring to the boil, stirring. Pour over poussins.

◆ Cover the cooking pot and cook on HIGH for 4-6 hours, or until poussins are cooked and tender. Remove poussins from the cooking pot, place on a plate and keep hot.

◆ In a small pan, blend cornflour with a little water. Stir in red wine sauce from the cooking pot, then bring to the boil, stirring, until thickened. Simmer gently for 3 minutes, stirring.

◆ Serve poussins with wine and leek sauce spooned over. Garnish with fresh coriander sprigs and serve with creamy mashed potatoes and stir-fried green vegetables, if desired.

Curried Turkey with Coconut

2 TABLESPOONS OLIVE OIL

1 ONION, CHOPPED

2 GARLIC CLOVES, CRUSHED

1 GREEN PEPPER, SEEDED AND THINLY SLICED

500G (1LB 2OZ) SKINLESS BONELESS TURKEY MEAT, CUT INTO SMALL DICE

1 TEASPOON GROUND CORIANDER

1 TEASPOON GROUND CUMIN

4 TEASPOONS THAI GREEN CURRY PASTE

115G (4OZ) GREEN BEANS, HALVED

175G (6OZ) BABY SWEETCORN, HALVED

300ML (10FL OZ) CHICKEN STOCK

150ML (5FL OZ) COCONUT MILK

2 TABLESPOONS CORNFLOUR

2-3 TABLESPOONS CHOPPED FRESH CORIANDER

TOASTED FLAKED COCONUT, TO GARNISH

◆ Preheat the slow cooker on HIGH while preparing ingredients. Heat oil in a pan, add onion, garlic, pepper and turkey and sauté for about 5 minutes, or until turkey is sealed all over, stirring occasionally.

◆ Add coriander, cumin and curry paste and cook for 1 minute, stirring. Add beans, sweetcorn, stock and coconut milk and stir to mix.

◆ In a small bowl, blend cornflour with a little water, add to curry and stir well to mix. Bring to the boil, stirring, then transfer to cooking pot.

◆ Cover, reduce the temperature to LOW and cook for 6-8 hours, or until turkey is cooked and tender.

◆ Stir in chopped coriander and garnish with toasted flaked coconut. Serve with plain boiled rice, if desired.

Braised Duck with Orange

SERVES 4

25G (1OZ) BUTTER

4 DUCK PORTIONS, SKINNED

2 RED ONIONS, THINLY SLICED

225G (8OZ) CHESTNUT MUSHROOMS, SLICED

2 TABLESPOONS PLAIN FLOUR

SEEDS FROM 4 CARDAMOM PODS, CRUSHED

175ML (6FL OZ) CHICKEN STOCK

150ML (5FL OZ) RED WINE

GRATED ZEST AND JUICE 1 ORANGE

2 TABLESPOONS ORANGE MARMALADE

SALT AND GROUND BLACK PEPPER

FRESH HERB SPRIGS, TO GARNISH

◆ Preheat the slow cooker on HIGH while preparing ingredients. Melt butter in a pan. Add duck and cook until lightly browned all over, turning occasionally. Transfer to the cooking pot using a slotted spoon and set aside.

◆ Add onions and mushrooms to the pan and sauté for 5 minutes. Stir in flour and cardamom and cook for 1 minute, stirring. Gradually stir in stock and wine, then add orange zest and juice, marmalade and seasoning.

◆ Bring to boil, stirring, then pour over duck in the cooking pot. Cover and cook on HIGH for 3-5 hours, or until duck is cooked and tender.

◆ Garnish with fresh herb sprigs and serve with boiled new potatoes, mangetout and baby sweetcorn, if desired.

Variation
Use chicken in place of duck portions.

Venison Casserole

SERVES 4-6

2 TABLESPOONS SUNFLOWER OIL

700G (1½LB) LEAN STEWING
VENISON, CUT INTO SMALL DICE

2 RED ONIONS, THINLY SLICED

4 CARROTS, THINLY SLICED

3 STICKS CELERY, THINLY SLICED

3 TABLESPOONS PLAIN FLOUR

225ML (8FL OZ) GAME
OR CHICKEN STOCK

200ML (7FL OZ) RED WINE

2 TABLESPOONS CRANBERRY SAUCE

1 TABLESPOON CHOPPED
FRESH THYME

200G (7OZ) BUTTON MUSHROOMS

115G (4OZ) DRIED CRANBERRIES

SALT AND GROUND BLACK PEPPER

FRESH HERB SPRIGS, TO GARNISH

Variation
Use lean braising or stewing beef in
place of venison.

◆ Preheat the slow cooker on HIGH while preparing ingredients. Heat oil in a large pan, add venison and cook until sealed all over, stirring occasionally. Transfer to cooking pot using a slotted spoon. Set aside.

◆ Add onions, carrots and celery to the pan and sauté for 5 minutes. Stir in flour and cook for 1 minute, stirring. Gradually stir in stock and wine, then add cranberry sauce, chopped thyme, mushrooms, dried cranberries and seasoning and bring to the boil, stirring.

◆ Transfer to the cooking pot and stir to mix well. Cover, reduce the temperature to LOW and cook for 8-10 hours, or until venison is cooked and tender.

◆ Garnish with fresh herb sprigs and serve with mustard-flavoured mashed potatoes and broccoli florets, if desired.

Meat

Beef with Raisins and Pine Nuts

SERVES 4

85ML (3FL OZ) OLIVE OIL

900G (2LB) LEAN BRAISING STEAK,
CUT INTO SMALL DICE

1 LARGE ONION, CHOPPED

1 GARLIC CLOVE, CHOPPED

225G (8OZ) BUTTON MUSHROOMS,
HALVED IF LARGE

1 RED PEPPER, SEEDED AND DICED

1 TABLESPOON CHOPPED
FRESH THYME

1 TABLESPOON CHOPPED FRESH
ROSEMARY

2 TABLESPOONS SEASONED PLAIN
FLOUR

2 TEASPOONS PAPRIKA

1 TEASPOON CINNAMON

150ML (5FL OZ) BEER

400G (14OZ) CAN CHOPPED
TOMATOES

2 BAY LEAVES

250ML (9FL OZ) BEEF STOCK

55G (2OZ) PINE NUTS

55G (2OZ) RAISINS

◆ Preheat the slow cooker on HIGH while preparing ingredients. Heat half the oil in a non-stick frying pan and fry meat over a medium heat for 4-5 minutes until lightly browned. Use a slotted spoon to transfer beef to cooking pot.

◆ Heat remaining oil in pan and sauté onion, garlic, mushrooms, pepper, thyme and rosemary for 5 minutes. Stir in flour, paprika and cinnamon and cook for 1 minute, stirring. Stir in beer, then add tomatoes, bay leaves and stock and bring to the boil, stirring.

◆ Pour over beef in cooking pot and stir to mix. Cover, reduce the temperature to LOW and cook for 7-9 hours.

◆ Stir in pine nuts and raisins, cover and cook on LOW for a further 1-2 hours, or until beef is cooked and tender.

◆ Serve with baked potatoes and broccoli florets, if desired.

Beef Tagine with Prunes

225G (8OZ) PITTED DRIED PRUNES

1 TEASPOON GROUND GINGER

1 TEASPOON GROUND CORIANDER

PINCH SAFFRON THREADS

SALT AND GROUND BLACK PEPPER

3 TABLESPOONS OLIVE OIL

1.25KG (2½LB) LEAN STEWING BEEF, CUT INTO SMALL DICE

2 ONIONS, THINLY SLICED

2 GARLIC CLOVES, CRUSHED

1 TABLESPOON PLAIN FLOUR

450ML (16FL OZ) BEEF STOCK OR WATER

1 CINNAMON STICK

1 TABLESPOON CLEAR HONEY

1 TEASPOON HARISSA PASTE

1 TABLESPOON SESAME SEEDS

3 TABLESPOONS CHOPPED FRESH PARSLEY

1 TEASPOON ORANGE FLOWER WATER, TO SERVE

◆ Place prunes in a bowl and cover with boiling water. Leave to soak for 2 hours.

◆ Preheat the slow cooker on HIGH. In a large bowl, mix together ginger, coriander, saffron, salt and pepper and 2 tablespoons of olive oil. Add beef and mix well, rubbing spices into meat with your fingers.

◆ In a large frying pan, heat remaining oil. Add beef and cook until sealed all over. Transfer to cooking pot using a slotted spoon. Set aside.

◆ Add onions and garlic to pan and sauté for 5 minutes. Stir in flour and cook for 1 minute, stirring. Stir in stock or water and bring to the boil, stirring, then add cinnamon stick. Pour over beef and stir to mix. Cover, reduce temperature to LOW and cook for 7-9 hours.

◆ Drain prunes and stir into beef mixture with honey and harissa paste. Cover and cook on LOW for a further 1-2 hours.

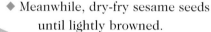

◆ Meanwhile, dry-fry sesame seeds until lightly browned.

◆ To serve, stir in parsley, sprinkle with orange flower water and scatter sesame seeds on top. Serve with couscous, if desired.

Beef Goulash with Chilli

2 TABLESPOONS OLIVE OIL

700G (1½LB) LEAN STEWING
OR BRAISING STEAK,
CUT INTO SMALL CUBES

1 ONION, SLICED

1 GARLIC CLOVE, CRUSHED

500G (1LB 2OZ) POTATOES, PEELED
AND CUT INTO SMALL CUBES

2 GREEN PEPPERS, SEEDED
AND THINLY SLICED

1 FRESH GREEN CHILLI, SEEDED
AND THINLY SLICED

2 TABLESPOONS PLAIN FLOUR

1 TABLESPOON PAPRIKA

300ML (10FL OZ) BEEF STOCK

400G (14OZ) CAN
CHOPPED TOMATOES

2 TABLESPOONS TOMATO PURÉE

PINCH CARAWAY SEEDS

2 BAY LEAVES

SALT AND GROUND BLACK PEPPER

◆ Preheat the slow cooker on HIGH while preparing ingredients. Heat oil in a pan, add beef and cook until meat is sealed all over, stirring occasionally. Transfer to cooking pot using a slotted spoon. Set aside.

◆ Add onion, garlic, potatoes, peppers and chilli to the pan and sauté for about 5 minutes, or until slightly softened.

◆ Stir in flour and paprika and cook for 1 minute, stirring. Gradually stir in stock, then add tomatoes, tomato purée, caraway seeds, bay leaves and seasoning and mix well. Bring to the boil, stirring, then transfer to the cooking pot and stir to mix.

◆ Cover, reduce temperature to LOW and cook for 10-12 hours, or until beef is cooked and tender.

◆ Remove and discard bay leaves and adjust seasoning. Serve with fresh bread or cooked noodles or rice, if desired.

Curried Pot-roast Beef

SERVES 6

2 TEASPOONS TURMERIC

2 TEASPOONS GROUND CORIANDER

2 TEASPOONS GROUND CUMIN

1 TEASPOON HOT CHILLI POWDER

1 TEASPOON GARAM MASALA

SALT AND GROUND BLACK PEPPER

1.35KG (3LB) LEAN BEEF JOINT
SUCH AS TOPSIDE

3 TABLESPOONS SUNFLOWER OIL

8 SHALLOTS, SLICED

4 CARROTS, THINLY SLICED

4 STICKS CELERY, THINLY SLICED

1 SWEDE, CUT INTO SMALL DICE

500-600ML (18-21FL OZ)
BEEF STOCK

2 TABLESPOONS CORNFLOUR

◆ Preheat the slow cooker on HIGH while preparing ingredients. In a small bowl, mix together turmeric, coriander, cumin, chilli powder, garam masala, salt and pepper. Rub spice mixture all over beef.

◆ Heat 2 tablespoons oil in a non-stick frying pan, add beef and cook quickly, turning frequently, until lightly browned and sealed all over. Transfer to the cooking pot.

◆ Heat remaining oil in the pan, add shallots, carrots, celery and swede and sauté for 5 minutes. Spoon vegetables around beef. Add stock to the pan, gently scraping up sediments in pan using a wooden spoon and bring to the boil.

◆ Pour enough stock into cooking pot to just cover vegetables. Cover, reduce temperature to LOW and cook for 6-8 hours or until beef is cooked and tender, turning beef and stirring once.

◆ Remove beef, place on a plate, cover and keep hot. Transfer vegetables to a saucepan.

◆ In a small bowl, blend cornflour with a little water until smooth. Stir into vegetable mixture, then bring to boil, stirring, until thickened. Simmer gently for 3 minutes.

◆ Slice beef and spoon vegetables over. Serve with plain boiled rice, if desired.

Beef with Paprika and Potatoes

SERVES 4

3 TABLESPOONS OLIVE OIL

700G (1½LB) LEAN STEWING BEEF, CUT INTO SMALL CUBES

2 ONIONS, CHOPPED

1 GARLIC CLOVE, CRUSHED

1 RED PEPPER, SEEDED AND THINLY SLICED

450G (1LB) POTATOES, PEELED AND DICED

2 TABLESPOONS PLAIN FLOUR

2 TABLESPOONS PAPRIKA

2-3 TABLESPOONS CARAWAY SEEDS

2 TABLESPOONS TOMATO PURÉE

350ML (12FL OZ) BEEF OR VEGETABLE STOCK

SALT AND GROUND BLACK PEPPER

150ML (5FL OZ) SOUR CREAM

◆ Preheat the slow cooker on HIGH while preparing ingredients. Heat 2 tablespoons oil in a large saucepan, add beef and cook until sealed all over. Transfer to cooking pot using a slotted spoon.

◆ Heat remaining oil in pan, add onions, garlic, red pepper and potatoes and sauté for 5 minutes. Add flour, paprika and caraway seeds and cook for 1 minute, stirring.

◆ Add tomato purée, stock and seasoning. Bring to the boil, then pour over beef and stir to mix. Cover, reduce temperature to LOW and cook for 10-12 hours, or until beef is cooked and tender.

◆ Pour over sour cream and stir to give a marbled effect. Cover and heat through on LOW for 20-30 minutes. Serve with fresh bread or cooked rice or noodles, if desired.

Pork, Potato and Fennel Casserole

SERVES 6

1.25KG (2½LB) LEAN PORK
TENDERLOIN OR BONELESS PORK
SHOULDER, CUT INTO SMALL DICE

1 TEASPOON CHOPPED FRESH THYME

1 TEASPOON FENNEL SEEDS,
CRUSHED

2 GARLIC CLOVES, CHOPPED

450ML (16FL OZ) MEDIUM-BODIED
DRY WHITE WINE

2 FENNEL BULBS

SEASONED PLAIN FLOUR

115G (4OZ) PIECE PANCETTA,
CUT INTO THIN STRIPS

3 TABLESPOONS VIRGIN OLIVE OIL

2 ONIONS, THINLY SLICED

700G (1½LB) SMALL
NEW POTATOES

SALT AND GROUND BLACK PEPPER

TOPPING

1½ TEASPOONS FINELY GRATED
LEMON ZEST

½ GARLIC CLOVE, FINELY CHOPPED

2 TABLESPOONS CHOPPED
FRESH PARSLEY

FEATHERY FENNEL FRONDS,
CHOPPED (SEE METHOD)

◆ Mix pork with thyme, fennel seeds, garlic and wine in a non-metallic dish. Cover and chill for at least 4 hours, or overnight, stirring occasionally.

◆ Preheat the slow cooker on HIGH. Trim and reserve feathery fronds of fennel bulbs, then cut each bulb into 6 wedges. Set aside.

◆ Lift pork from marinade, reserving marinade. Pat pork dry on absorbent kitchen paper and coat lightly with seasoned flour.

◆ Fry pancetta in 2 tablespoons oil in a large pan until lightly browned and fat runs. Transfer to cooking pot using a slotted spoon. Set aside.

◆ Add onions, fennel bulb wedges and potatoes to pan and sauté for 5 minutes. Add to cooking pot.

◆ Add remaining oil to pan, add pork and cook until sealed all over. Stir in marinade and seasoning, bring to the boil and bubble for 2 minutes.

◆ Transfer pork to cooking pot and stir to mix. Cover the cooking pot, reduce temperature to LOW and cook for 8-10 hours, or until pork is cooked and tender.

◆ To make topping, in a small bowl mix together lemon zest, garlic, parsley and reserved fennel fronds. Scatter over casserole to serve. Serve with cooked fresh vegetables such as baby carrots and green beans, if desired.

Braised Pork with Cabbage and Apples

SERVES 4

1 TABLESPOON OLIVE OIL

25G (1OZ) BUTTER

4 LEAN LOIN PORK CHOPS

1 LARGE ONION, THINLY SLICED

3 STICKS CELERY, FINELY CHOPPED

2 TABLESPOONS PLAIN FLOUR

250ML (9FL OZ) CHICKEN
OR VEGETABLE STOCK

250ML (9FL OZ) DRY
OR MEDIUM CIDER

350G (12OZ) WHITE CABBAGE,
SHREDDED

1 LARGE COOKING APPLE, PEELED,
CORED AND SLICED

1 TEASPOON DRIED SAGE

SALT AND GROUND BLACK PEPPER

FRESH HERB SPRIGS, TO GARNISH

◆ Preheat the slow cooker on HIGH while preparing ingredients. Heat oil and butter in a pan. Add chops and cook until sealed all over, turning once. Transfer to the cooking pot using a slotted spoon and set aside.

◆ Add onion and celery to the pan and sauté for 5 minutes. Stir in flour and cook for 1 minute, stirring. Gradually stir in stock and cider, then bring to the boil, stirring.

◆ Add cabbage, apple, sage and seasoning and stir to mix. Pour mixture over chops. Cover, reduce the temperature to LOW and cook for 6-8 hours, or until pork is cooked and tender.

◆ Garnish with fresh herb sprigs. Serve with mashed potatoes and vegetables such as peas, if desired.

Variation
Use fresh or dried thyme in place of dried sage.

Paprika Pork and Bean Casserole

SERVES 4-6

225G (8OZ) DRIED HARICOT OR
BLACK-EYE BEANS,
SOAKED OVERNIGHT

40G (1½OZ) BUTTER

700G (1½LB) LEAN PORK
TENDERLOIN OR BONELESS PORK
SHOULDER, CUT INTO SMALL CUBES

1 ONION, CHOPPED

1 GARLIC CLOVE, CRUSHED

2 LEEKS, THINLY SLICED

2 STICKS CELERY, SLICED

3 CARROTS, THINLY SLICED

25G (1OZ) PLAIN FLOUR

1 TABLESPOON PAPRIKA

300ML (10FL OZ) CHICKEN
OR VEGETABLE STOCK

200ML (7FL OZ) DRY
OR MEDIUM CIDER

227G (8OZ) CAN
CHOPPED TOMATOES

1 TABLESPOON TOMATO PURÉE

SALT AND GROUND
BLACK PEPPER

1 BOUQUET GARNI

SOUR CREAM,
TO SERVE (OPTIONAL)

◆ Preheat the slow cooker on HIGH while preparing ingredients. Drain beans, place in a large pan and cover with fresh cold water. Bring to the boil and boil for 10 minutes. Rinse, drain and set aside.

◆ Meanwhile, melt butter in a pan, add meat and cook until sealed all over. Transfer to the cooking pot using a slotted spoon and set aside.

◆ Add onion, garlic, leeks, celery and carrots to the pan and sauté for 5 minutes. Stir in flour and paprika and cook for 1 minute, stirring. Gradually stir in stock and cider, then add tomatoes, tomato purée, beans and seasoning.

◆ Bring to the boil, stirring, then add bouquet garni. Transfer to the cooking pot and stir to mix. Cover, reduce the temperature to LOW and cook for 8-10 hours, or until pork is cooked and tender.

◆ Remove and discard bouquet garni. Top each portion with 1 tablespoon sour cream and serve with sautéed potatoes and broccoli florets, if desired.

Cook's Tip
Top each portion with 1 tablespoon sour cream to serve, if desired.

t and Sour Meatballs

500G (1LB 2OZ) LEAN MINCED PORK

4 SHALLOTS, FINELY CHOPPED

115G (4OZ) MUSHROOMS, FINELY CHOPPED

55G (2OZ) FRESH BREADCRUMBS

3 TABLESPOONS SUN-DRIED TOMATO PURÉE

FINELY GRATED ZEST 1 LEMON

2 TEASPOONS DRIED HERBES DE PROVENCE

SALT AND GROUND BLACK PEPPER

2 TABLESPOONS PLAIN FLOUR

2 TABLESPOONS OLIVE OIL

1 TABLESPOON CORNFLOUR

4 TABLESPOONS RED WINE

300ML (10FL OZ) PASSATA

150ML (5FL OZ) UNSWEETENED APPLE JUICE

2 TABLESPOONS RED WINE VINEGAR

2 TABLESPOONS LIGHT SOFT BROWN SUGAR

◆ Place minced pork, shallots, mushrooms, breadcrumbs, 2 tablespoons tomato purée, lemon zest, dried herbs and seasoning in a bowl and mix well.

◆ Divide mixture into 28 equal portions and roll each into a small ball. Roll meatballs in flour, place on a plate and chill in the refrigerator for 20 minutes.

◆ Preheat the slow cooker on HIGH. Heat oil in a frying pan, add meatballs and fry for about 10 minutes, or until lightly browned all over, turning occasionally.

◆ Meanwhile, blend cornflour with red wine in a pan. Stir in passata, apple juice, vinegar, sugar and remaining 1 tablespoon tomato purée. Heat gently, stirring continuously, until mixture comes to the boil and thickens. Simmer gently for 3 minutes.

◆ Transfer meatballs to the cooking pot using a slotted spoon and pour sauce over the top. Cover, reduce temperature to LOW and cook for 6-8 hours or until meatballs are cooked and tender.

◆ Serve with egg noodles or rice and stir-fried vegetables, if desired.

Variations
Use tomato juice in place of passata.
Use pineapple or orange juice in place of apple juice.

Spicy Sausage and Mushroom Hotpot

SERVES 4-6

8 THICK SPICY PREMIUM
PORK SAUSAGES

2 TABLESPOONS SUNFLOWER OIL

1 RED ONION, THINLY SLICED

1 GARLIC CLOVE, CRUSHED

1 FRESH RED CHILLI,
SEEDED AND FINELY CHOPPED

2 PARSNIPS, DICED

2 CARROTS, THINLY SLICED

2 STICKS CELERY, THINLY SLICED

350G (12OZ) CHESTNUT
MUSHROOMS, SLICED

2 TABLESPOONS PLAIN FLOUR

250ML (9FL OZ) VEGETABLE STOCK

200ML (7FL OZ) PASSATA
OR TOMATO JUICE

2 TEASPOONS CHILLI SAUCE

SALT AND GROUND BLACK PEPPER

700G (1½LB) PEELED
POTATOES, THINLY SLICED

15G (½OZ) BUTTER,
MELTED

◆ Preheat the slow cooker on HIGH while preparing ingredients. Grill sausages until lightly browned all over. Cut each sausage into 3 pieces and set aside.

◆ Meanwhile, heat oil in a pan, add onion, garlic, chilli, parsnips, carrots, celery and mushrooms and sauté for 5 minutes.

◆ Stir in flour and cook for 1 minute, stirring. Gradually add stock and passata or tomato juice, then add chilli sauce and seasoning. Bring to the boil, stirring.

◆ Put one third of the vegetable mixture in the cooking pot, then arrange one third of the potato slices over the top. Place half the sausages on top of potatoes. Continue layering vegetables, potatoes and sausages, finishing with a layer of potatoes.

◆ Cover the cooking pot, reduce the temperature to LOW and cook for 8-10 hours, or until cooked.

◆ Brush top layer of potatoes with melted butter and place under a preheated grill until golden. Serve with runner beans and baby sweetcorn, if desired.

Hungarian Goulash

3 TABLESPOONS VEGETABLE OIL

2 LARGE ONIONS, THINLY SLICED

2 GARLIC CLOVES, THINLY SLICED

*1 LARGE GREEN PEPPER, SEEDED
AND THINLY SLICED*

2 TABLESPOONS PLAIN FLOUR

1½ TABLESPOONS PAPRIKA

*900G (2LB) BONELESS PORK
SHOULDER, CUT INTO SMALL DICE*

300ML (10FL OZ) RED WINE

*400G (14OZ) CAN CHOPPED
TOMATOES*

*450G (1LB) BUTTON MUSHROOMS,
SLICED*

1 TEASPOON DRIED THYME

2 BAY LEAVES

◆ Preheat the slow cooker on HIGH while preparing ingredients. Heat 2 tablespoons of the oil in a large pan and sauté onions, garlic and green pepper for 5 minutes. Transfer to the cooking pot. Set aside.

◆ Mix flour and paprika together and coat pork with this mixture. Add remaining oil to the pan, then cook pork quickly for 5 minutes to brown all over.

◆ Add wine, tomatoes, mushrooms, thyme, bay leaves and salt and pepper and bring to the boil, stirring. Transfer to the cooking pot and stir to mix.

◆ Cover, reduce temperature to LOW and cook for 8-10 hours or until pork is cooked and tender

◆ Serve goulash with cooked noodles or rice or with fresh crusty bread, if desired.

Stifado

85ML (3FL OZ) VEGETABLE OIL

900G (2LB) ONIONS, CHOPPED

4 GARLIC CLOVES, CHOPPED

*900G (2LB) LEAN STEWING BEEF,
CUT INTO SMALL DICE*

2 TABLESPOONS PLAIN FLOUR

*900G (2LB) PLUM TOMATOES,
PEELED AND CHOPPED*

3 TABLESPOONS TOMATO PURÉE

350ML (12FL OZ) RED WINE

◆ Preheat the slow cooker on HIGH while preparing ingredients. Heat 3 tablespoons of the oil in a large pan. Add onions and garlic and sauté for 5 minutes. Transfer to the cooking pot.

◆ Heat remaining oil in the pan, add beef and cook until sealed all over. Stir in flour and cook for 1 minute, stirring. Add tomatoes, tomato purée, wine and seasoning and bring to the boil, stirring.

◆ Transfer to the cooking pot and stir to mix. Cover, reduce temperature to LOW and cook for 8-10 hours, or until beef is cooked and tender.

◆ Serve with fresh crusty bread, if desired.

Fragrant Gammon

SERVES 6-8

1.25-1.35KG (2½-3LB)
GAMMON JOINT

225G (8OZ) PARSNIPS,
QUARTERED LENGTHWAYS

450G (1LB) CARROTS,
CUT INTO SMALL CHUNKS

450G (1LB) SWEDE,
CUT INTO SMALL CHUNKS

2 STICKS CELERY,
CUT INTO SMALL CHUNKS

450ML (16FL OZ) MEDIUM OR
DRY CIDER OR VEGETABLE STOCK

1 TABLESPOON BROWN SUGAR

1 TABLESPOON RED WINE VINEGAR

1 TABLESPOON BLACK PEPPERCORNS

6 CLOVES

OREGANO SPRIGS, TO GARNISH

◆ Put gammon in a large pan, cover with cold water and leave to soak for 1-2 hours.

◆ Preheat the slow cooker on HIGH. Drain gammon, return to the pan and cover with fresh water. Bring to the boil, then rinse, drain and place in the cooking pot.

◆ Add parsnips, carrots, swede, celery, cider or stock, sugar, vinegar, peppercorns and cloves to the cooking pot. Cover and cook on HIGH for 4-6 hours or until gammon and vegetables are cooked and tender.

◆ Lift out gammon, slice and arrange on warmed serving plates. Remove vegetables with a slotted spoon and arrange around gammon. Garnish with oregano sprigs and serve.

Lamb and Apricot Tagine

SERVES 4-6

2 TABLESPOONS OLIVE OIL

700G (1½LB) LEAN BONELESS LEG OR SHOULDER OF LAMB, CUT INTO SMALL CUBES

1 LARGE ONION, THINLY SLICED

2 GARLIC CLOVES, CRUSHED

4 CARROTS, THINLY SLICED

1 TABLESPOON PLAIN FLOUR

1 TEASPOON TURMERIC

1 TEASPOON GROUND CORIANDER

1 TEASPOON GROUND CUMIN

1 TEASPOON GROUND CINNAMON

SALT AND GROUND BLACK PEPPER

450ML (16FL OZ) LAMB OR VEGETABLE STOCK

225G (8OZ) BUTTON MUSHROOMS

GRATED ZEST 1 LEMON

175G (6OZ) READY-TO-EAT DRIED APRICOTS, CHOPPED

2 TABLESPOONS CLEAR HONEY

CHOPPED FRESH CORIANDER, TO SERVE (OPTIONAL)

◆ Preheat the slow cooker on HIGH while preparing ingredients. Heat oil in a pan, add lamb and cook in batches until sealed all over. Transfer to the cooking pot using a slotted spoon and set aside.

◆ Add onion, garlic and carrots to the pan and sauté for 5 minutes. Stir in flour, turmeric, coriander, cumin, cinnamon, salt and pepper. Cook for 1 minute, stirring.

◆ Gradually add stock, then add mushrooms and lemon zest and bring to the boil, stirring. Transfer to the cooking pot and stir to mix. Cover, reduce the temperature to LOW and cook for 6-8 hours.

◆ Stir in apricots and honey, cover and cook on LOW for a further 1-2 hours, or until lamb is cooked and tender.

◆ Sprinkle with chopped fresh coriander and serve with couscous and green beans or okra, if desired.

Lamb and Pepper Hotpot

SERVES 4

2 TABLESPOONS SUNFLOWER OIL

8 LEAN LOIN LAMB CHOPS

2 ONIONS, THINLY SLICED

2 RED PEPPERS, SEEDED AND SLICED

3 STICKS CELERY, THINLY SLICED

4 CARROTS, THINLY SLICED

3 BAKING POTATOES,
PEELED AND THINLY SLICED

350ML (12FL OZ) LAMB
OR VEGETABLE STOCK

2 TABLESPOONS TOMATO PURÉE

2 TEASPOONS DRIED MIXED HERBS

SALT AND GROUND BLACK PEPPER

15G (½OZ) BUTTER, MELTED

FRESH HERB SPRIGS, TO GARNISH
(OPTIONAL)

◆ Preheat the slow cooker on HIGH while preparing ingredients. Heat oil in a pan, add lamb chops and cook in batches until sealed all over. Transfer to a plate and set aside.

◆ Add onions, peppers, celery and carrots to the pan and sauté for 5 minutes.

◆ Place 4 lamb chops in the base of the cooking pot. Arrange one third of the potato slices over lamb and top potatoes with half the vegetable mixture. Repeat these layers and finish with a layer of potato slices.

◆ Mix stock, tomato purée, mixed herbs, salt and pepper and pour into the cooking pot over lamb and vegetables.

◆ Cover, reduce temperature to LOW and cook for 8-10 hours or until lamb and vegetables are cooked and tender.

◆ Brush top layer of potatoes with melted butter and place under a preheated grill until golden.

◆ Garnish with fresh herb sprigs to serve.

Note
This recipe is best cooked in a slow cooker with a minimum capacity of 4.5-5 litres (4.5-5 quarts).

Vegetarian Dishes

Vegetable Biryani

3 TABLESPOONS SUNFLOWER OIL

*300G (10OZ) CARROTS,
FINELY CHOPPED*

*115G (4OZ) PEELED POTATOES,
CUT INTO SMALL CUBES*

450G (1LB) ONIONS, THINLY SLICED

*2.5CM (1IN) PIECE FRESH GINGER,
PEELED AND GRATED*

2 GARLIC CLOVES, CRUSHED

1 TABLESPOON HOT CURRY PASTE

1 TEASPOON TURMERIC

½ TEASPOON GROUND CINNAMON

*225G (8OZ) AMERICAN
EASY-COOK LONG-GRAIN RICE*

750ML (27FL OZ) VEGETABLE STOCK

SALT AND GROUND BLACK PEPPER

*115G (4OZ) SMALL
CAULIFLOWER FLORETS*

*115G (4OZ) FRESH
SHELLED PEAS*

*55G (2OZ) TOASTED
CASHEW NUTS*

*2 TABLESPOONS
CHOPPED FRESH
CORIANDER*

◆ Preheat the slow cooker on HIGH, while preparing ingredients. Heat 2 tablespoons oil in a pan and add carrots, potatoes and half the onions. Stir in ginger and garlic and sauté for 10 minutes.

◆ Add curry paste, turmeric, cinnamon and rice and cook, stirring, for 1 minute. Pour in stock and bring to boil. Season with salt and pepper. Transfer to the cooking pot, cover and cook on HIGH for 1 hour.

◆ Meanwhile, cook cauliflower and peas in a pan of boiling water for 5 minutes. Drain. Stir cauliflower, peas and cashew nuts into rice mixture, adding a little extra stock if needed. Cover and cook on HIGH for a further 30-60 minutes, or until rice is cooked and tender and liquid has been absorbed.

◆ Meanwhile, heat remaining oil in a pan. Add reserved onions and cook, stirring occasionally, for 10-15 minutes, until crisp and golden. Remove with a slotted spoon, drain on kitchen paper and set aside.

◆ Stir coriander into biryani and scatter reserved crisp onions over to serve.

Stuffed Peppers

SERVES 4

*4 LARGE PEPPERS
(ASSORTED COLOURS)*

2 TABLESPOONS OLIVE OIL

4 SHALLOTS, FINELY CHOPPED

1 GARLIC CLOVE, CRUSHED

*115G (4OZ) MUSHROOMS,
FINELY CHOPPED*

1 COURGETTE, FINELY CHOPPED

175G (6OZ) COOKED BROWN RICE

*2 TOMATOES, SKINNED,
SEEDED AND FINELY CHOPPED*

*55G (2OZ) PINE NUTS,
FINELY CHOPPED*

*55G (2OZ) PITTED BLACK OLIVES,
FINELY CHOPPED*

*2 TABLESPOONS CHOPPED
FRESH MIXED HERBS*

SALT AND GROUND BLACK PEPPER

150ML (5FL OZ) VEGETABLE STOCK

◆ Preheat the slow cooker on HIGH while preparing ingredients. Slice tops off peppers and remove and discard cores and seeds. Cook peppers and lids in a pan of boiling water for 5 minutes. Drain and set aside.

◆ Heat oil in a pan, add shallots, garlic, mushrooms and courgette and sauté for 5 minutes.

◆ Remove pan from the heat and add rice, tomatoes, pine nuts, olives, herbs, salt and pepper. Stir well to combine.

◆ Spoon some rice stuffing into each pepper and top with lids. Place peppers in the cooking pot. Heat stock in a pan until boiling, then pour it around peppers.

◆ Cover and cook on HIGH for 2-4 hours, or until peppers are tender.

◆ Serve with fresh crusty bread and a mixed baby leaf salad, if desired.

Potato and Bean Casserole with Tomatoes

SERVES 4

225G (8OZ) HARICOT BEANS,
SOAKED OVERNIGHT AND DRAINED

2 TABLESPOONS OLIVE OIL

450G (1LB) BABY NEW POTATOES,
HALVED, OR POTATOES,
CUT INTO SMALL CHUNKS

1 LARGE ONION, CHOPPED

2 LEEKS, SLICED

2 GARLIC CLOVES, CHOPPED

1 TEASPOON CUMIN SEEDS

1 TEASPOON PAPRIKA

227G (8OZ) CAN CHOPPED
TOMATOES

2 TABLESPOONS TOMATO PURÉE

350ML (12FL OZ)
VEGETABLE STOCK

2 TABLESPOONS CHOPPED
FRESH CORIANDER

SALT AND GROUND BLACK PEPPER

GREEK-STYLE YOGURT, TO SERVE

◆ Preheat the slow cooker on HIGH. Boil beans in a pan with sufficient water to cover for 10 minutes. Rinse and drain beans and set aside.

◆ Meanwhile, heat oil in a large pan, add potatoes, onion and leeks and sauté for 5 minutes.

◆ Stir in garlic, cumin and paprika and sauté for 1 minute. Add tomatoes, tomato purée, stock and beans. Bring to the boil.

◆ Transfer to the cooking pot, cover and reduce temperature to LOW. Cook for 8-12 hours, or until beans are cooked and tender.

◆ Stir in coriander and salt and pepper to taste. Serve with yogurt and a mixed green salad, if desired.

Root Vegetable Curry

SERVES 4

2 TABLESPOONS OLIVE OIL

1 RED ONION, CHOPPED

2 GARLIC CLOVES, CRUSHED

*1 FRESH RED CHILLI,
SEEDED AND FINELY CHOPPED*

*2.5CM (1IN) PIECE FRESH GINGER,
PEELED AND FINELY CHOPPED*

*700G (1½LB) PREPARED MIXED
ROOT VEGETABLES, SUCH AS
SWEET POTATO, POTATO, CARROTS,
CELERIAC AND SWEDE,
CUT INTO SMALL DICE*

2 TABLESPOONS PLAIN FLOUR

2 TEASPOONS GROUND TURMERIC

2 TEASPOONS GROUND CORIANDER

2 TEASPOONS GROUND CUMIN

*350ML (12FL OZ)
VEGETABLE STOCK*

150ML (5FL OZ) PASSATA

115G (4OZ) SULTANAS

SALT AND GROUND BLACK PEPPER

*2-3 TABLESPOONS CHOPPED
FRESH CORIANDER*

◆ Preheat slow cooker on HIGH while preparing ingredients. Heat oil in a large pan and sauté onion, garlic, chilli and ginger for 3 minutes.

◆ Add prepared root vegetables and sauté gently for 10 minutes.

◆ Stir in flour, turmeric, coriander and cumin and cook for 1 minute, stirring. Gradually stir in stock and passata, then add sultanas and salt and pepper.

◆ Bring to the boil, stirring, then transfer to the cooking pot. Cover, reduce the temperature to LOW and cook for 8-10 hours, or until vegetables are cooked and tender.

◆ Stir in chopped coriander. Serve with plain boiled rice, if desired.

Macaroni and Broccoli Bake

225G (8OZ) DRIED MACARONI

225G (8OZ) SMALL BROCCOLI FLORETS

85G (3OZ) BUTTER

225G (8OZ) LEEKS, THINLY SLICED

55G (2OZ) PLAIN FLOUR

950ML (30FL OZ) MILK

175G (6OZ) CHEDDAR CHEESE, GRATED

1 TEASPOON PREPARED ENGLISH MUSTARD

340G (12OZ) CAN SWEETCORN KERNELS, DRAINED

SALT AND GROUND BLACK PEPPER

25G (1OZ) FRESH BREADCRUMBS

25G (1OZ) FINELY GRATED FRESH PARMESAN CHEESE

2 TABLESPOONS CHOPPED FRESH CHIVES

◆ Preheat the slow cooker on HIGH while preparing ingredients. Cook macaroni in a pan of boiling water for 8 minutes, or until just tender. Add broccoli to the pan for the last 3 minutes of cooking time. Drain well and set aside.

◆ Meanwhile, melt 25g (1oz) butter in a pan, add leeks and sauté for 8-10 minutes, or until softened. Place on a plate and set aside.

◆ Add remaining butter to the pan with flour and milk and heat gently, whisking continuously, until sauce comes to the boil and thickens. Simmer gently for 3 minutes, stirring.

◆ Remove the pan from the heat and stir in cheese until it has melted. Add macaroni, broccoli, leeks, mustard, sweetcorn and seasoning and mix well.

◆ Grease the cooking pot. Transfer macaroni mixture to the cooking pot. Cover, reduce the temperature to LOW and cook for 3-4 hours.

◆ Preheat the grill to high. Combine breadcrumbs, Parmesan and chopped chives and sprinkle evenly over macaroni bake. Grill until golden.

◆ Serve with grilled tomatoes, if desired.

Spicy Root Vegetable Casserole

SERVES 4-6

2 TABLESPOONS OLIVE OIL

1 ONION, THINLY SLICED

1 GARLIC CLOVE, CRUSHED

3 STICKS CELERY, THINLY SLICED

225G (8OZ) CARROTS,
THINLY SLICED

225G (8OZ) PEELED SWEDE,
CUT INTO SMALL DICE

175G (6OZ) PEELED PARSNIPS,
CUT INTO SMALL DICE

225G (8OZ) PEELED POTATOES,
CUT INTO SMALL DICE

2 TEASPOONS GROUND CORIANDER

2 TEASPOONS GROUND CUMIN

2 TEASPOONS HOT CHILLI POWDER

175G (6OZ) PUY OR GREEN
LENTILS, RINSED AND DRAINED

400G (14OZ) CAN CHOPPED
TOMATOES

700ML (25FL OZ)
VEGETABLE STOCK

SALT AND GROUND BLACK PEPPER

2 TABLESPOONS CHOPPED
FRESH CORIANDER

◆ Preheat the slow cooker on HIGH while preparing ingredients. Heat oil in a large pan, add onion, garlic and celery and sauté for 3 minutes.

◆ Add carrots, swede, parsnips and potatoes and sauté for 5 minutes.

◆ Add coriander, cumin and chilli powder and cook for 1 minute, stirring. Add lentils, tomatoes, stock and seasoning and stir to mix. Bring to the boil, stirring, then transfer to the cooking pot.

◆ Cover and cook on HIGH for 3-4 hours or until vegetables and lentils are cooked and tender.

◆ Stir in coriander and serve with fresh crusty bread, if desired.

Variation
Use sweet potatoes in place of standard potatoes.

Oriental-style Ratatouille

4 TABLESPOONS OLIVE OIL

1 SMALL ONION, FINELY CHOPPED

2 GARLIC CLOVES, FINELY CHOPPED

450G (1LB) RIPE PLUM TOMATOES,
PEELED AND CHOPPED

2 TABLESPOONS TAMARI
(JAPANESE SOY SAUCE)

1½ TABLESPOONS RICE WINE
OR DRY SHERRY

2 TABLESPOONS VEGETABLE STOCK

1 TEASPOON SUGAR

SALT AND GROUND BLACK PEPPER

1 FRESH GREEN CHILLI,
SEEDED AND FINELY CHOPPED

2 TEASPOONS CORIANDER SEEDS,
TOASTED AND CRUSHED

1 SMALL AUBERGINE, DICED

150G (5OZ) SHIITAKE MUSHROOMS,
SLICED

2 SMALL COURGETTES,
CUT INTO DIAGONAL SLICES

1 YELLOW AND 1 RED PEPPER,
CORED, SEEDED AND THINLY SLICED

2 TEASPOONS SESAME SEEDS,
TOASTED

◆ Preheat the slow cooker on HIGH while preparing ingredients. Heat 2 tablespoons of oil in a saucepan. Gently sauté onion for 5 minutes.

◆ Add garlic and fry for 30 seconds. Stir in tomatoes, tamari, rice wine or sherry, stock and sugar. Season with salt and pepper to taste. Simmer over a low heat for 2 minutes, stirring occasionally. Set aside.

◆ Heat remaining oil in a large pan and sauté chilli and coriander seeds for 1-2 minutes.

◆ Add aubergine, mushrooms, courgettes and peppers to the pan and sauté for 5 minutes.

◆ Stir in reserved tomato sauce and bring to the boil. Transfer to the cooking pot.

◆ Cover, reduce temperature to LOW and cook for 4-8 hours, or until vegetables are cooked to your liking.

◆ Adjust seasoning to taste and stir in sesame seeds. Serve with warm crusty bread and a mixed dark leaf salad, if desired.

Vegetable Chilli Bake

SERVES 4

2 TABLESPOONS SUNFLOWER OIL

6 SHALLOTS, SLICED

2 GARLIC CLOVES, CRUSHED

3 STICKS CELERY, FINELY CHOPPED

1 GREEN PEPPER,
SEEDED AND DICED

1 LARGE FRESH GREEN CHILLI,
SEEDED AND FINELY CHOPPED

3 CARROTS, THINLY SLICED

175G (6OZ) PEELED TURNIP
OR SWEDE, CUT INTO SMALL CUBES

2 TEASPOONS GROUND CUMIN

1 TEASPOON HOT CHILLI POWDER

400G (14OZ) CAN CHOPPED
TOMATOES

2 TABLESPOONS TOMATO PURÉE

200ML (7FL OZ) VEGETABLE STOCK

225G (8OZ) CHESTNUT
MUSHROOMS, SLICED

410G (14½OZ) CAN RED KIDNEY
BEANS, RINSED AND DRAINED

SALT AND GROUND BLACK PEPPER

1 TABLESPOON CORNFLOUR

FRESH HERB SPRIGS, TO GARNISH

◆ Preheat the slow cooker on HIGH while preparing ingredients. Heat oil in a pan, add shallots, garlic, celery, green pepper and chilli and sauté for 3 minutes.

◆ Add carrots and turnip or swede and sauté for 5 minutes. Add ground cumin and chilli powder and cook for 1 minute, stirring.

◆ Add tomatoes, tomato purée, stock, mushrooms, kidney beans and seasoning and stir to mix. In a small bowl, blend cornflour with a little water, then stir it into vegetable mixture.

◆ Bring to the boil, stirring, then transfer to the cooking pot. Cover, reduce the temperature to LOW and cook for 6-8 hours, or until vegetables are cooked and tender.

◆ Garnish with fresh herb sprigs and serve with cooked rice, if desired.

Fruit and Nut Pilaf

SERVES 4

1 TABLESPOON OLIVE OIL

1 ONION, FINELY CHOPPED

2 GARLIC CLOVES, CRUSHED

1 FRESH RED CHILLI,
SEEDED AND FINELY CHOPPED

1 RED PEPPER, SEEDED AND DICED

1½ TEASPOONS GROUND CORIANDER

1½ TEASPOONS GROUND CUMIN

225G (8OZ) AMERICAN
EASY-COOK LONG-GRAIN RICE

115G (4OZ) SULTANAS

115G (4OZ) READY-TO-EAT
DRIED APRICOTS, CHOPPED

750ML (27FL OZ)
VEGETABLE STOCK

3 TABLESPOONS DRY SHERRY

SALT AND GROUND BLACK PEPPER

115G (4OZ) UNSALTED CASHEW
NUTS, TOASTED

2 TABLESPOONS CHOPPED FRESH
CORIANDER

FRESH CORIANDER SPRIGS,
TO GARNISH (OPTIONAL)

◆ Preheat the slow cooker on HIGH while preparing ingredients. Heat oil in a pan, add onion, garlic, chilli and red pepper and sauté for 5 minutes.

◆ Add coriander, cumin and rice and cook for 1 minute, stirring. Add sultanas, apricots, stock, sherry and seasoning and mix well.

◆ Bring to the boil, stirring, then transfer to the cooking pot. Cover and cook on HIGH for 1-2 hours, or until rice is cooked and tender and all liquid has been absorbed. Stir once halfway through cooking time and add a little extra hot stock, if needed.

◆ Stir in cashew nuts and chopped coriander. Garnish with fresh coriander and serve with a green salad, if desired.

Chickpea and Aubergine Casserole

SERVES 6

1 TEASPOON CUMIN SEEDS

2 TEASPOONS CORIANDER SEEDS

2 TABLESPOONS SESAME SEEDS

2 TEASPOONS DRIED OREGANO

25G (1OZ) SHELLED BRAZIL NUTS
OR ALMONDS, TOASTED

3 TABLESPOONS OLIVE OIL

2 ONIONS, FINELY CHOPPED

1 RED PEPPER, SEEDED AND DICED

1 AUBERGINE, DICED

225G (8OZ) GREEN BEANS,
CHOPPED

2 GARLIC CLOVES, CRUSHED

1/2 TEASPOON HOT CHILLI POWDER,
OR TO TASTE

400G (14OZ) CAN CHOPPED
TOMATOES

420G (15OZ) CAN CHICKPEAS,
DRAINED

200ML (7FL OZ) VEGETABLE STOCK

SALT

3 TABLESPOONS FINELY CHOPPED
FRESH CORIANDER

YOGURT, TO SERVE

◆ Preheat the slow cooker on HIGH while preparing ingredients. Dry-fry cumin, coriander and sesame seeds together in a heavy-based pan until the aroma rises. Add oregano and fry for a few more seconds.

◆ Put seeds, oregano and nuts in a blender and grind to a powder.

◆ Heat oil in a large pan. Add onions, pepper, aubergine and green beans and sauté for 5 minutes. Add garlic, ground seed mixture and chilli powder and cook for 2 minutes, stirring.

◆ Add tomatoes, chickpeas and stock. Bring to the boil, season with a little salt, then transfer to cooking pot. Cover, reduce temperature to LOW and cook for 7-9 hours, or until vegetables are cooked and tender.

◆ Check seasoning, adding more salt or chilli powder if necessary. Stir in coriander and serve with yogurt.

Harvest Vegetable Hotpot

SERVES 4-6

2 TABLESPOONS SUNFLOWER OIL

6 SHALLOTS, SLICED

2 LEEKS, SLICED

2 STICKS CELERY, FINELY CHOPPED

1 RED PEPPER, SEEDED AND SLICED

*500G (1LB 2OZ) PREPARED MIXED
ROOT VEGETABLES, SUCH AS
CARROTS, PARSNIPS AND SWEDE OR
TURNIP, CUT INTO SMALL CUBES*

*225G (8OZ) SMALL CAULIFLOWER
FLORETS, HALVED*

*400G (14OZ) CAN CHOPPED
TOMATOES*

150ML (5FL OZ) VEGETABLE STOCK

*150ML (5FL OZ) DRY WHITE WINE
OR CIDER*

*2 TEASPOONS DRIED
HERBES DE PROVENCE*

SALT AND GROUND BLACK PEPPER

2 TABLESPOONS CORNFLOUR

*500G (1LB 2OZ) PEELED POTATOES,
THINLY SLICED*

15G (½OZ) BUTTER, MELTED

*FRESH HERB SPRIGS,
TO GARNISH*

◆ Preheat the slow cooker on HIGH while preparing ingredients. Heat oil in a large pan and sauté shallots, leeks and celery for 5 minutes.

◆ Add red pepper, root vegetables and cauliflower and sauté for a further 5 minutes. Add tomatoes, stock, wine or cider, dried herbs and seasoning and mix well.

◆ In a small bowl, blend cornflour with a little water, then stir into vegetable mixture. Bring to the boil, stirring continuously, until mixture thickens. Simmer gently for 2 minutes, stirring.

◆ Spoon one third of the vegetable mixture into the cooking pot, then arrange one third of the potato slices over vegetables. Repeat these layers twice more, finishing with a neat layer of potatoes on top.

◆ Cover, reduce the temperature to LOW and cook for 6-8 hours, or until vegetables are cooked and tender.

◆ Brush the top with melted butter and place under a preheated grill until golden. Garnish with fresh herb sprigs. Serve with green beans, if desired.

Cheesy Courgette Strata

SERVES 4-6

25G (1OZ) BUTTER

1 ONION, FINELY CHOPPED

1 SMALL LEEK, THINLY SLICED

2 COURGETTES, SLICED

200G (7OZ) CAN SWEETCORN
KERNELS, DRAINED

SALT AND GROUND BLACK PEPPER

9 MEDIUM SLICES OF BREAD,
CRUSTS REMOVED AND SLICES
CUT INTO FINGERS

3 MEDIUM EGGS

550ML (20FL OZ) MILK

2 TABLESPOONS CHOPPED
FRESH CHIVES

2 TABLESPOONS CHOPPED
FRESH PARSLEY

115G (4OZ) MATURE CHEDDAR
CHEESE, GRATED

◆ Preheat the slow cooker on HIGH while preparing ingredients. Grease a 1.75-2 litre (2¾-3 pint) ovenproof soufflé or similar dish and set aside.

◆ Melt butter in a pan, add onion, leek and courgettes and sauté for 8-10 minutes or until softened. Remove pan from the heat and stir in sweetcorn and seasoning. Set aside.

◆ Place one third of bread in the base of the prepared dish. Top with half the courgette mixture. Repeat layers, ending with a layer of bread.

◆ Heat milk in a small pan or in a microwave. Whisk together eggs, hot milk, chopped chives and parsley and seasoning, then pour into the dish over bread and vegetables.

◆ Sprinkle cheese over the top. Cover loosely with greased aluminium foil. Place in the cooking pot of the slow cooker.

◆ Add sufficient boiling water to the cooking pot to come halfway up the sides of the dish. Cover and cook on HIGH for 3-4 hours (or on LOW for 4-6 hours) or until lightly set.

◆ Serve with broccoli and cauliflower florets or a mixed leaf salad, if desired.

Desserts

Chocolate Fondue

350G (12OZ) PLAIN CHOCOLATE

40G (1½OZ) BUTTER

225ML (8FL OZ) DOUBLE CREAM

½ TEASPOON GROUND CINNAMON

3 TABLESPOONS BRANDY OR RUM

FOR DIPPING

SELECTION OF PREPARED FRESH
FRUIT (SUCH AS STRAWBERRIES,
CHERRIES, KIWI FRUIT AND BANANA)

SPONGE FINGERS
OR SWEET WAFER BISCUITS

READY-TO-EAT DRIED FRUITS
(SUCH AS APRICOTS AND FIGS)

WHOLE NUTS
(SUCH AS WALNUTS OR BRAZIL NUTS)

◆ Break chocolate into squares. Place chocolate squares in the cooking pot of the slow cooker with butter, cream, cinnamon and brandy or rum. Stir to mix.

◆ Cover and cook on LOW for 1-2 hours, or until all ingredients have melted together, stirring once.

◆ Stir briskly until well combined and smooth, then serve with fresh and dried fruits, sponge fingers and nuts for dipping.

Apricot Bread Pudding

SERVES 4-6

40G (1½OZ) BUTTER, SOFTENED

6 MEDIUM SLICES OF BREAD,
CRUSTS REMOVED

175G (6OZ) READY-TO-EAT
DRIED APRICOTS, FINELY CHOPPED

40G (1½OZ) LIGHT SOFT
BROWN SUGAR

2 TEASPOONS GROUND MIXED SPICE

3 LARGE EGGS

450ML (16FL OZ) SINGLE CREAM

◆ Preheat the slow cooker on HIGH while preparing ingredients. Lightly grease a 1.5-1.75 litre (2¾-3 pint) ovenproof soufflé or similar dish that will sit in your cooking pot.

◆ Spread butter over bread slices, then cut bread into small triangles or fingers. Arrange half of the bread in the base of the prepared dish, butter-side up.

◆ Mix together apricots, sugar and mixed spice and sprinkle over bread. Top with remaining bread, butter-side up.

◆ Beat eggs and cream together and pour over bread. Set aside for 30 minutes to allow bread to absorb some of the liquid.

◆ Cover with greased aluminium foil, then place in the cooking pot. Add sufficient boiling water to come halfway up the sides of the dish. Cover the cooking pot, reduce the temperature to LOW and cook for 3-5 hours or until custard has set.

◆ Serve with fresh fruit, such as sliced peaches, nectarines or apricots, if desired.

Variations
Use sultanas or ready-to-eat dried pears in place of apricots. Use ground cinnamon or ginger in place of mixed spice.

Fresh Lemon Sponge Pudding

4 TABLESPOONS GOLDEN SYRUP

115G (4OZ) BUTTER (SOFTENED)
OR MARGARINE

115G (4OZ) LIGHT SOFT
BROWN SUGAR

2 MEDIUM EGGS

FINELY GRATED ZEST 1 LEMON

175G (6OZ) SELF-RAISING FLOUR,
SIFTED

2-3 TABLESPOONS MILK

◆ Preheat the slow cooker on HIGH while preparing ingredients. Lightly grease a 1-litre (1¾-pint) pudding basin and line the base with a small circle of non-stick baking parchment. Spoon syrup into the base of the prepared basin and set aside.

◆ In a bowl, beat butter or margarine and sugar together until pale and creamy. Gradually beat in eggs, then beat in lemon zest. Fold in flour and add enough milk to make a soft, dropping consistency.

◆ Spoon mixture into the basin over syrup and level the surface. Cover loosely with a double layer of greased aluminium foil and place in the cooking pot of the slow cooker.

◆ Add sufficient boiling water to the cooking pot to come halfway up the sides of the basin. Cover and cook on HIGH for 3-4 hours or until sponge is cooked and a skewer inserted in the centre comes out clean.

◆ Carefully turn out onto a warmed serving plate. Serve with custard, cream or ice cream, if desired.

Christmas Pudding

SERVES 8-10

175G (6OZ) RAISINS

175G (6OZ) SULTANAS

55G (2OZ) DRIED CRANBERRIES

55G (2OZ) READY-TO-EAT
DRIED APRICOTS, FINELY CHOPPED

2 TABLESPOONS BRANDY OR SHERRY

FINELY GRATED ZEST
AND JUICE 1 SMALL ORANGE

FINELY GRATED ZEST
AND JUICE 1 LEMON

55G (2OZ) PLAIN FLOUR

2 TEASPOONS GROUND MIXED SPICE

115G (4OZ) FRESH BREADCRUMBS

115G (4OZ) SHREDDED BEEF
OR VEGETABLE SUET

115G (4OZ) LIGHT SOFT
BROWN SUGAR

3 MEDIUM EGGS,
BEATEN

◆ Put raisins, sultanas and dried cranberries and apricots in a bowl, add brandy or sherry and orange and lemon zest and stir to mix well. Cover and leave to soak for several hours or overnight.

◆ Preheat the slow cooker on HIGH while preparing pudding. Lightly grease a 1.3-1.4-litre (2¼-2½-pint) pudding basin and line the base with a small circle of non-stick baking parchment.

◆ Mix flour, mixed spice, breadcrumbs, suet and sugar in a bowl. Add dried fruits and soaking liquid and eggs and beat together until mixed. Spoon mixture into the prepared basin and level the surface.

◆ Cover with a sheet of non-stick baking parchment and cover this with a double layer of pleated aluminium foil. Secure with string. Place in the cooking pot of the slow cooker.

◆ Add sufficient boiling water to the cooking pot to come three-quarters of the way up the sides of the basin. Cover and cook on HIGH for 8-12 hours, or until pudding is cooked, topping up with boiling water as necessary.

◆ Turn pudding out onto a warmed serving plate and serve immediately. Alternatively, allow to cool, then re-cover and store in a cool, dry place until required.

Chocolate Sponge Cake

SERVES 8-10

175G (6OZ) BUTTER, SOFTENED

175G (6OZ) LIGHT SOFT
BROWN SUGAR

3 MEDIUM EGGS, BEATEN

175G (6OZ) SELF-RAISING FLOUR

25G (1OZ) COCOA POWDER

FEW DROPS VANILLA ESSENCE

1-2 TABLESPOONS MILK

150ML (5FL OZ) DOUBLE OR
WHIPPING CREAM (OPTIONAL)

ICING SUGAR, FOR SIFTING
(OPTIONAL)

◆ Preheat the slow cooker on HIGH. Lightly grease and line an 18cm (7in) round deep cake tin. Cream butter and sugar together in a bowl until lightly fluffy, then gradually beat in eggs. Sift in flour and cocoa powder and fold in lightly with vanilla essence. Add enough milk to make a soft dropping consistency.

◆ Spoon into tin and level surface. Cover loosely with greased aluminium foil. Stand the tin on top of a crumpet ring or plain metal pastry cutter in cooking pot of slow cooker. Add sufficient boiling water to come halfway up sides of tin. Cover and cook on HIGH for 2-3 hours, or until a skewer inserted in centre of cake comes out clean.

◆ Lift tin out of the slow cooker and leave to stand for 5 minutes. Turn cake out of the tin and leave to cool completely on a wire rack. Fill with whipped cream and sift over icing sugar to serve, if desired.

Moist Cider Cake

SERVES 8-10

300G (10OZ) MIXED DRIED FRUIT

2 TABLESPOONS MIXED PEEL

250ML (9FL OZ) MEDIUM CIDER

115G (4OZ) BUTTER, DICED

175G (6OZ) LIGHT SOFT
BROWN SUGAR

115G (4OZ) SIEVED COOKED
POTATOES

225G (8OZ) PLAIN FLOUR

2 TEASPOONS GROUND MIXED SPICE

1 TEASPOON BICARBONATE OF SODA

1 MEDIUM EGG, BEATEN

◆ Soak dried fruit and mixed peel in cider in a non-metallic bowl overnight. Preheat the slow cooker on HIGH. Lightly grease and line an 18cm (7in) round deep cake tin.

◆ Transfer soaked fruit mixture to a saucepan and add butter and sugar. Bring to boil slowly, stirring occasionally. Simmer for 10 minutes.

◆ Remove from heat, leave to cool slightly, then mix in potatoes, flour, mixed spice, bicarbonate of soda and beaten egg to give a very soft dropping consistency. Pour mixture into tin and level surface. Cover loosely with greased aluminium foil.

◆ Stand tin on top of a metal pastry cutter in cooking pot. Add boiling water to come halfway up sides of tin. Cover and cook on HIGH for 5-7 hours, or until a skewer inserted in centre of cake comes out clean.

◆ Lift tin out of slow cooker and leave to stand for 5 minutes. Turn cake out of tin and leave to cool completely on a wire rack.

Tipsy Pears

SERVES 4

4 LARGE CONFERENCE PEARS

425ML (15FL OZ) RED WINE

*150ML (5FL OZ) UNSWEETENED
APPLE JUICE*

*85G (3OZ) LIGHT SOFT
BROWN SUGAR*

2 CINNAMON STICKS

4 WHOLE CLOVES

FRESH MINT SPRIGS, TO DECORATE

◆ Preheat the slow cooker on HIGH while preparing ingredients. Carefully peel pears, then cut them in half and remove and discard cores. Place in the cooking pot and set aside.

◆ Place red wine, apple juice and sugar in a saucepan and heat gently, stirring, until sugar has dissolved. Add cinnamon sticks and cloves, then bring to the boil.

◆ Pour over pears in the cooking pot. Cover, reduce the temperature to LOW and cook for 6-8 hours or until pears are tender.

◆ Carefully remove pears from liquid and keep hot. Remove and discard cinnamon sticks and cloves.

◆ Pour liquid into a pan and boil rapidly until it is reduced and thickened slightly. Spoon liquid over pears and decorate with fresh mint sprigs. Serve warm or cold with crème fraîche or yogurt, if desired.

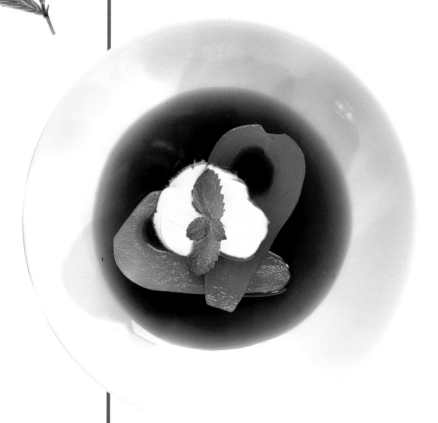

Rice Pudding with Orange

SERVES 4-6

25g (1oz) butter

85g (3oz) pudding rice, rinsed and drained

85g (3oz) caster sugar

675ml (24fl oz) milk

225ml (8fl oz) evaporated milk

Finely grated zest 1 large orange

Seeds from 3 cardamom pods, crushed

Pared orange rind, to decorate

◆ Grease the inside of the cooking pot of the slow cooker with a little butter.

◆ Place rice, sugar, milk, evaporated milk, orange zest and crushed cardamom seeds in the cooking pot and stir to mix. Dot with any remaining butter.

◆ Cover and cook on HIGH for 3-4 hours (or on LOW for 4-6 hours), or until the rice is cooked and most of the liquid has been absorbed. Stir once or twice during the final 2 hours of cooking, if possible.

◆ Decorate with pared orange rind. Serve with stewed fresh fruit, such as plums, or warm fruit compote, if desired.

Crème Caramel

SERVES 4-6

175G (6OZ) CASTER SUGAR

4 MEDIUM EGGS

½ TEASPOON VANILLA ESSENCE

550ML (20FL OZ) MILK

◆ Preheat the slow cooker on HIGH while preparing crème caramel. Grease an 18cm (7in) soufflé dish or similar ovenproof dish. Set aside.

◆ Put 115g (4oz) sugar in a small pan with 150ml (5fl oz) water. Heat gently, stirring, until sugar has dissolved, then bring to the boil and boil without stirring, until mixture caramelises to a golden brown. Pour into the prepared dish and set aside.

◆ Put eggs, vanilla essence and remaining sugar in a bowl and whisk together lightly. Set aside.

◆ Warm milk in a saucepan, then pour onto egg mixture, whisking continuously. Strain over cooled caramel. Cover the dish with aluminium foil, then place in the cooking pot of the slow cooker.

◆ Add sufficient boiling water to the cooking pot to come halfway up the sides of the dish. Cover, reduce temperature to LOW and cook for 5-6 hours or until set (a knife inserted in the centre should come out clean when it is cooked).

◆ Remove the dish from the slow cooker, uncover and leave to cool, then chill for several hours.

◆ Gently ease dessert away from the sides of the dish and carefully turn out onto a serving plate. Serve with fresh fruit, such as raspberries, if desired.

Winter Fruit Compote

SERVES 6

175G (6OZ) READY-TO-EAT
DRIED APRICOTS

55G (2OZ) DRIED APPLE RINGS

115G (4OZ) READY-TO-EAT
DRIED PRUNES

55G (2OZ) SULTANAS

55G (2OZ) RAISINS

1 PEAR, PEELED, CORED
AND CUT INTO 8

2 CINNAMON STICKS

THINLY PARED RIND 1 LEMON

600ML (21FL OZ)
UNSWEETENED APPLE JUICE

FRESH MINT SPRIGS, TO DECORATE

Variations
Use your own choice of mixed dried
fruits in similar proportions to
above, if preferred.

◆ Preheat the slow cooker on HIGH for 15-20 minutes. Put dried apricots, apple rings, prunes, sultanas, raisins and pear in cooking pot. Add cinnamon sticks, lemon rind and apple juice and stir gently to mix.

◆ Cover, reduce the temperature to LOW and cook for 8-10 hours or until fruit is plumped up and tender.

◆ Remove and discard cinnamon sticks and lemon rind. Decorate with mint sprigs.

◆ Serve compote warm or cold, with crème fraîche, mascarpone cheese or Greek-style yogurt, if desired.

Index